BECOME A WINNER RIGHT NOW

In the same series

Become Your Best Self Right Now

Make Your Life Extraordinary Right Now

Become Successful Right Now

Empower Yourself Right Now

BECOME A WINNER RIGHT NOW

A MASTERCLASS FROM THE

SUPERGURUS

ALEPH

ALEPH

ALEPH BOOK COMPANY
An independent publishing firm
promoted by *Rupa Publications India*

First published in India in 2024
by Aleph Book Company
7/16 Ansari Road, Daryaganj
New Delhi 110 002

ISBN: 978-81-19635-30-6

1 3 5 7 9 10 8 6 4 2

Printed in India

Contents

Introduction   vii

SECTION I
HOW TO WIN AT LIFE

1. Aspiration: James Allen   3
2. Nothing Is Humdrum: Arnold Bennett   7
3. The Major Decision of Your Life: Dale Carnegie   11
4. Imagination: The Workshop of the Mind:
   Napoleon Hill   19
5. The Dignity of Self-reliance: William George Jordan   23
6. Possibilities in Spare Moments:
   Orison Swett Marden   29
7. Just What Is the Secret of Power?: Earl Prevette   34
8. In All Matters Affecting Our Weal or Woe,
   We Should Be: Arthur Schopenhauer   39
9. The Discipline of Experience: Samuel Smiles   44
10. The Flower at My Window: Lucian B. Watkins   51

SECTION II
ACCUMULATING WEALTH

11. Eight Pillars: James Allen   55
12. How to Lesson Your Financial Worries:
    Dale Carnegie   60
13. Seven Cures to a Lean Purse: George Clason   68
14. On Buying and Selling: Kahlil Gibran   87
15. Success: Henry Thomas Hamblin   89

16. Specialized Knowledge, Personal Experience, or
    Observations: Napoleon Hill   94
17. Hurry, the Scourge of America:
    William George Jordan   101
18. Making Yourself a Prosperity Magnet:
    Orison Swett Marden   106
19. How to Turn Your Ability into Cash: Earl Prevette   112
20. Work: Samuel Smiles   116

SECTION III
DEALING WITH HARDSHIP

21. Serenity: James Allen   125
22. A Picture: Olivia Ward Bush-Banks   128
23. Don't Let the Beetles Get You Down: Dale Carnegie 130
24. 'Hope' Is the Thing with Feathers: Emily Dickinson 138
25. Overcoming Life's Difficulties:
    Henry Thomas Hamblin   139
26. Success under Difficulties: Orison Swett Marden   143
27. How to Receive Guidance from Your Subconscious:
    Joseph Murphy   148
28. It Might Have Been You: Earl Prevette   151
29. Influence of Character: Samuel Smiles   159
30. Work and Its Secrets: Swami Vivekananda   165

Notes on Contributors   171

Introduction

In the hustle of fast-paced lives, the pursuit of 'success' often seems like an elusive goal, especially when its definition has become constricted to the acquisition of tangible and monetary achievements. Trapped in this relentless chase for more, individuals tend to lose sight of what it means to experience true happiness and stability, both prerequisites for enduring success. We forget that a feeling of triumph doesn't always need to stem from grand feats. Even the smallest acts of kindness, resilience, and service can be an act of winning. However, it is not always easy to incorporate such principles. More often than not, we blindly compare our lives to others whom we think are 'winning' in the most conventional sense of the term—a disheartening habit that, in the long run, will prevent us from unlocking our true potential, for it forces us to visualize winning in the narrowest possible ways.

This is where supergurus make their entrance. These immensely charismatic, wise, and learned men and women have spent their lives exploring existential questions integral to the human experience, and in the process, have discovered secrets that have proved to be tremendously beneficial for millions seeking illumination and solace. The supergurus understand how success, fulfillment, and progress mean different things to different people. So instead of pushing one and all towards an identical destination, their extensive experience in the field of psychological development ensures that their profound insights can be molded to fit each person's reality and bring about radical empowerment in a way that helps people gain success that is lasting, sustainable, and wholesome. They don't speak in abstractions or offer solutions that are out of reach for the common man and woman. Their answers are easy to implement, and most importantly, deeply considerate of the fact that 'winning' is not just the acquisition of material wealth but a feeling of all-encompassing happiness that can be experienced in myriad ways.

The anthology contains thirty essays, divided into three sections that take the reader on a transformative journey. The first section, How to Win at Life, delves into the power of optimism, creativity, and reaching out for what you deserve. The second section, Accumulating Wealth, provides practical pointers on maximizing wealth and inculcating fiscal responsibility. The final section, Dealing with Hardship, draws on the wisdom of experts to help readers navigate the big and small trials and tribulations of daily life. Taken together, the essays serve as a beacon of light in a complex world, showing us that there is profound joy to be found in moments of quiet relaxation, in small milestones, in the fulfillment of a seemingly humdrum task, and in the beauty of everyday tasks—all these are different forms of accomplishment.

Become a Winner Right Now is not just a compilation of motivational clichés but a carefully curated collection that distills the essence of what it means to be an achiever from those who have walked the path. When engaged with an open mind, the wisdom gathered together between the pages will make you a winner in every sense of the term.

SECTION I

HOW TO WIN AT LIFE

James Allen

From Passion to Peace

James Allen, a renowned British thinker and writer, wrote several celebrated inspirational tracts and poems. The following excerpt, Aspiration, from his book From Passion to Peace, *speaks of the importance of consistently working towards a higher plane of existence where an individual imbibes wisdom and purity in their thoughts and frees themselves of the desire for material gains.*

~

ASPIRATION

With clear perception of one's own ignorance comes the desire for enlightenment, and thus in the heart is born aspiration, the rapture of the saints.

On the wings of aspiration man rises from earth to heaven, from ignorance to knowledge, from the under darkness to the upper light. Without it he remains a grovelling animal, earthly, sensual, unenlightened, and uninspired.

Aspiration is the longing for heavenly things—for righteousness, compassion, purity, love—as distinguished from desire, which is the longing for earthly things—for selfish possessions, personal dominance, low pleasures, and sensual gratifications.

As a bird deprived of its wings cannot soar, so a man without aspiration cannot rise above his surroundings and become master of his animal inclinations. He is the slave of passions, is subject to others, and is carried hither and thither by the changing current of events.

For one to begin to aspire means that he is dissatisfied with his low status, and is aiming at a higher condition. It is a sure sign that he is aroused out of his lethargic sleep of animality, and has become conscious of nobler attainments and a fuller life.

Aspiration makes all things possible. It opens the way to advancement. Even the highest state of perfection conceivable it brings near and makes real and possible; for that which can be conceived can be achieved.

So long as animal conditions taste sweet to a man, he cannot aspire; he is already satisfied. But when their sweetness turns to bitterness, then in his sorrow he thinks of nobler things. When he is deprived of earthly joy, he aspires to the joy which is heavenly. It is when impurity turns to suffering that purity is sought. Truly aspiration rises, phoenix-like, from the dead ashes of repentance, but on its powerful pinions man can reach the heaven of heavens.

The man of aspiration has entered the way which ends in peace, and surely he will reach that end if he neither stays nor turns back. If he constantly renews his mind with glimpses of the heavenly vision, he will reach the heavenly state.

Man attains in the measure that he aspires. His longing to be is the gauge of what he can be. To fix the mind is to foreordain the achievement. As man can experience and know all low things, so he can experience and know all high things. As he has become human, so can he become divine. The turning of the mind in high and divine directions is the sole and needful task.

What is impurity but the impure thoughts of the thinker? What is purity but the pure thoughts of the thinker? One man does not do the thinking of another. Each man is pure or impure of himself alone.

If a man thinks, 'It is through others, or circumstances, or heredity that I am impure,' how can he hope to overcome his errors? Such a thought will check all holy aspirations and bind him to the slavery of passion.

When a man fully perceives that his errors and impurities are his own, that they are generated and fostered by himself, that he alone is responsible for them, then he will aspire to overcome them. The way of attainment will be opened up to him, and he will see from where and to what destination he is travelling.

The man of passion sees no straight path before him, and behind him is all fog and gloom. He seizes the pleasure of the moment and does not strive for understanding or think of wisdom. His way is confused, turbulent, and troubled, and his heart is far from peace.

The man of aspiration sees before him the pathway up the heavenly heights, and behind him are the circuitous routes of passion up which he has hitherto blindly groped. Striving for understanding, and his mind set on wisdom, his way is clear, and his heart already experiences a foretaste of the final peace.

Men of passion strive mightily to achieve little things— things which speedily perish, and, in the place where they were, leave nothing to be remembered.

Men of aspiration strive with equal might to achieve great things—things of virtue, of knowledge, of wisdom, which do not perish, but stand as monuments of inspiration for the uplifting of humankind.

Aspiration can be fed, fostered, and strengthened by daily habit, just as desire. It can be sought, and admitted into the mind as a divine guide, or it can be neglected and shut out. To retire for a short time each day to some quiet spot, preferably in the open air, and there call up the energies of the mind in surging waves of holy rapture, is to prepare the mind for great spiritual victories and destinies of divine import. For such a rapture is the preparation for wisdom and the prelude to peace.

Before the mind can contemplate pure things it must be lifted up to them, it must rise above impure things; and aspiration is the instrument by which this is accomplished. By its aid the mind soars swiftly and surely into heavenly places, and begins to experience divine things. It begins to accumulate wisdom, and to learn to guide itself by an ever-increasing measure of the divine light of pure knowledge.

To thirst for righteousness; to hunger for the pure life; to rise in holy rapture on the wings of angelic aspiration—this is the right road to wisdom. This is the right striving for peace. This is the right beginning of the way divine.

.2.

Arnold Bennett

How to Live on Twenty-Hours a Day

Of more than two dozen non-fiction books written by eminent British novelist Arnold Bennett, How to Live on Twenty-Hours a Day *has endured ever since its publication in 1908 because of its humorous yet powerful message of finding happiness in the ebbs and flows of everyday life. In this extract, the author urges the reader to be curious and explore the joys hidden in everyday life.*

~

NOTHING IS HUMDRUM

Art is a great thing. But it is not the greatest. The most important of all perceptions is the continual perception of cause and effect—in other words, the perception of the continuous development of the universe—in still other words, the perception of the course of evolution. When one has thoroughly got imbued into one's head the leading truth that nothing happens without a cause, one grows not only large-minded, but large-hearted.

It is hard to have one's watch stolen, but one reflects that the thief of the watch became a thief from causes of heredity and environment which are as interesting as they are scientifically comprehensible; and one buys another watch, if not with joy, at any rate with a philosophy that makes bitterness impossible. One loses, in the study of cause and effect, that absurd air which so many people have of being always shocked and pained by the curiousness of life. Such people live amid human nature as if human nature were a foreign country full of awful foreign customs. But, having reached maturity, one ought surely to be ashamed of being a stranger in a strange land!

The study of cause and effect, while it lessens the painfulness of life, adds to life's picturesqueness. The man to whom evolution is but a name looks at the sea as a grandiose, monotonous spectacle, which he can witness in August for three shillings third-class return. The man who is imbued with the idea of development, of continuous cause and effect, perceives in the sea an element which in the day-before-yesterday of geology was vapour, which yesterday was boiling, and which to-morrow will inevitably be ice.

He perceives that a liquid is merely something on its way to be solid, and he is penetrated by a sense of the tremendous, changeful picturesqueness of life. Nothing will afford a more durable satisfaction than the constantly cultivated appreciation of this. It is the end of all science.

Cause and effect are to be found everywhere. Rents went up in Shepherd's Bush. It was painful and shocking that rents should go up in Shepherd's Bush. But to a certain point we are all scientific students of cause and effect, and there was not a clerk lunching at a Lyons Restaurant who did not scientifically put two and two together and see in the (once) Two-penny Tube the cause of an excessive demand for wigwams in Shepherd's Bush, and in the excessive demand for wigwams the cause of the increase in the price of wigwams.

'Simple!' you say, disdainfully. Everything—the whole complex movement of the universe—is as simple as that— when you can sufficiently put two and two together. And, my dear sir, perhaps you happen to be an estate agent's clerk, and you hate the arts, and you want to foster your immortal soul, and you can't be interested in your business because it's so humdrum. Nothing is humdrum.

The tremendous, changeful picturesqueness of life is marvellously shown in an estate agent's office. What! There was a block of traffic in Oxford Street; to avoid the block people actually began to travel under the cellars and drains, and the result was a rise of rents in Shepherd's Bush! And you say that isn't picturesque! Suppose you were to study, in this spirit, the property question in London for an hour and a half every other evening. Would it not give zest to your business, and transform your whole life?

You would arrive at more difficult problems. And you would be able to tell us why, as the natural result of cause and effect, the longest straight street in London is about a yard and a half in length, while the longest absolutely straight street in Paris extends for miles. I think you will admit that in an estate agent's clerk I have not chosen an example that specially favours my theories.

You are a bank clerk, and you have not read that breathless romance (disguised as a scientific study), Walter Bagehot's *Lombard Street*? Ah, my dear sir, if you had begun with that, and followed it up for ninety minutes every other evening, how enthralling your business would be to you, and how much more clearly you would understand human nature.

You are 'penned in town,' but you love excursions to the country and the observation of wild life—certainly a heart-enlarging diversion. Why don't you walk out of your house door, in your slippers, to the nearest gas lamp of a night with a butterfly net, and observe the wild life of common and rare moths that is beating about it, and co-ordinate the knowledge thus obtained and build a superstructure on it, and at last get to know something about something?

You need not be devoted to the arts, not to literature, in order to live fully.

The whole field of daily habit and scene is waiting to satisfy that curiosity which means life, and the satisfaction of which means an understanding heart.

Dale Carnegie

How to Stop Worrying and Start Living

*Dale Carnegie's classic bestseller is one of the most widely-read
self-help books in the world. In this lesson, he shares easy-to-
implement pointers for young individuals struggling to
decide a career path for themselves. Utilizing his tips,
one can curb indecision and make substantial
progress towards choosing a vocation.*

~

THE MAJOR DECISION OF YOUR LIFE

If you are under eighteen, you will probably soon be called
upon to make the two most important decisions of your
life—decisions that will profoundly alter all the days of your
years: decisions that may have far-reaching effects upon your
happiness, your income, your health; decisions that may make
or break you.

What are these two tremendous decisions?

First: how are you going to make a living? Are you going
to be a farmer, a mail carrier, a chemist, a forest ranger, a
stenographer, a horse dealer, a college professor, or are you
going to run a hamburger stand?

Second: whom are you going to select to be the father or
mother of your children?

Both of those great decisions are frequently gambles.
'Every boy,' says Harry Emerson Fosdick in his book, *The*

Power to See It Through, 'every boy is a gambler when he chooses a vocation. He must stake his life on it'.

How can you reduce the gamble in selecting a vocation? Read on; we will tell you as best we can.

First, try, if possible, to find work that you enjoy. I once asked David M. Goodrich, chairman of the board, B. F. Goodrich Company (tyre manufacturers) what he considered the first requisite of success in business, and he replied: 'Having a good time at your work. If you enjoy what you are doing,' he said, 'you may work long hours, but it won't seem like work at all. It will seem like play.'

But how can you have enthusiasm for a job when you haven't the foggiest idea of what you want to do? 'The greatest tragedy I know of,' said Mrs Edna Kerr, who once hired thousands of employees for the Dupont Company, 'is that so many young people never discover what they really want to do. I think no one else is so much to be pitied as the person who gets nothing at all out of his work but his pay.' Mrs Kerr reports that even college graduates come to her and say: 'I have a B.A. degree from Dartmouth (or an M.A. from Cornell). Have you some kind of work I can do for your firm?' They don't know themselves what they are able to do, or even what they would like to do. Is it any wonder that so many men and women who start out in life with competent minds and rosy dreams end up at forty in utter frustration and even with a nervous breakdown?

I recently spent an evening with Paul W. Boynton, employment supervisor for the Socony Vacuum Oil Company. He has interviewed more than 75,000 people looking for jobs, and he has written a book entitled *6 Ways to Get a Job*. I asked him: 'What is the greatest mistake young people make today in looking for work?'

'They don't know what they want to do,' he said. 'It is

perfectly appalling to realise that a man will give more thought to buying a suit of clothes that will wear out in a few years than he will give to choosing the career on which his whole future depends—on which his whole future happiness and peace of mind are based!'

And so what? What can you do about it? You can take advantage of a new profession called vocational guidance. It may help you—or harm you—depending on the ability and character of the counsellor you consult. This new profession isn't even within gunshot of perfection yet. It hasn't even reached the Model T stage. But it has a great future. How can you make use of this science? By finding out where, in your community, you can get vocational tests and vocational advice.

Such advice can only take the form of suggestions. You have to make the decisions. Remember that these counsellors are far from infallible. They don't always agree with one another. They sometimes make ridiculous mistakes. For example, a vocational guidance counsellor advised one of my students to become a writer solely because she had a large vocabulary. How absurd! It isn't as simple as that. Good writing is the kind that transfers your thoughts and emotions to the reader—and to do that, you don't need a large vocabulary, but you do need ideas, experience, convictions, examples, and excitement. The vocational counsellor who advised this girl with a large vocabulary to become an author succeeded in doing only one thing: he turned an erstwhile happy stenographer into a frustrated, would-be novelist.

The point I am trying to make is that vocational guidance experts, even as you and I, are not infallible. Perhaps you had better consult several of them, and then interpret their findings in the sunlight of common sense.

You may think it strange that I am including a chapter

like this in a book devoted to worry. But it isn't strange at all, when you understand how many of our worries, regrets, and frustrations are spawned by work we despise. Ask your father about it—or your neighbour or your boss. No less an intellectual giant than John Stuart Mill declared that industrial misfits are 'among the heaviest losses of society'. Yes, and among the unhappiest people on this earth are those same 'industrial misfits' who hate their daily work!

Do you know the kind of man who 'cracked up' in the army? The man who was misplaced! I'm not talking about battle casualties, but about the men who cracked up in ordinary service. Dr William Menninger, one of our greatest living psychiatrists, was in charge of the Army's neuro-psychiatric division during the war, and he says: 'We learned much in the army as to the importance of selection and of placement, of putting the right man in the right job. A conviction of the importance of the job at hand was extremely important. Where a man had no interest, where he felt he was misplaced, where he thought he was not appreciated, where he believed his talents were being misused, invariably we found a potential if not an actual psychiatric casualty.'

Yes—and for the same reasons, a man may 'crack up' in industry. If he despises his business, he can crack it up, too.

Even at the risk of starting family rows, I would like to say to young people: don't feel compelled to enter a business or trade just because your family wants you to do it! Don't enter a career unless you want to do it! However, consider carefully the advice of your parents. They have probably lived twice as long as you have. They have gained the kind of wisdom that comes only from much experience and the passing of many years. But, in the last analysis, you are the one who has to make the final decision.

You are the one who is going to be either happy or miserable at your work. Now, having said this, let me give you the following suggestions—some of them warnings—about choosing your work:

1. Read and study the following five suggestions about selecting a vocational guidance counsellor. These suggestions are right from the horse's mouth. They were made by one of America's leading vocational guidance experts, Professor Harry Dexter Kitson of Columbia University.

    a) 'Don't go to anyone who tells you that he has a magic system that will indicate your 'vocational aptitude'. In this group are phrenologists, astrologers, 'character analysts', handwriting experts. Their "systems" do not work.'

    b) 'Don't go to anyone who tells you that he can give you a test that will indicate what occupation you should choose. Such a person violates the principle that a vocational counsellor must take into account the physical, social, and economic conditions surrounding the counselee; and he should render his service in the light of the occupational opportunities open to the counselee.'

    c) 'Seek a vocational counsellor who has an adequate library of information about occupation and uses it in the counselling process.'

    d) 'A thorough vocational guidance service generally requires more than one interview.'

    e) 'Never accept vocational guidance by mail.'

2. Keep out of business and professions that are already jam-packed and overflowing! There are many thousands of different ways of making a living. But do young people

know this? Not unless they hire a swami to gaze into a crystal ball. The result? In one school, two-thirds of the boys confined their choices to five occupations—five out of twenty thousand and four-fifths of the girls did the same. Small wonder that a few business and professions are overcrowded—small wonder that insecurity, worry, and 'anxiety neuroses' are rampant at times among the white-collar fraternity. Beware of trying to elbow your way into such overcrowded fields as law, journalism, radio, motion pictures, and the 'glamour occupations'.

3. Stay out of activities where the chances are only one out of ten of your being able to make a living. As an example, take selling life insurance. Each year countless thousands start out trying to sell life insurance without bothering to find out in advance what is likely to happen to them! Here is approximately what does happen, according to Franklin L. Bettger, Real Estate Trust Building, Philadelphia. For twenty years, Mr Bettger was one of the outstandingly successful insurance salesmen in America. He declares that ninety per cent of the men who start selling life insurance get so heartsick and discouraged that they give it up within a year. Out of the ten who remain, one man will sell ninety per cent of the insurance sold by the group of ten; and the other nine will sell only ten per cent. To put it another way: if you start selling life insurance, the chances are nine to one that you will fail and quit within twelve months, and the chances are only one in a hundred that you will make ten thousand a year out of it. Even if you remain at it, the chances are only one out of ten that you will be able to do anything more than barely scratch out a living.

4. Spend weeks—even months, if necessary—finding out all you can about an occupation before deciding to devote

your life to it! How? By interviewing men and women who have already spent ten, twenty, or forty years in that occupation.

To illustrate, let's suppose that you are thinking about studying to be an architect. Here is a list of questions I would like to ask you when speaking to professional architects:

- If you had your life to live over, would you become an architect again?
- After you have sized me up, I want to ask you whether you think I have what it takes to succeed as an architect.
- Is the profession of architecture overcrowded?
- I studied architecture for four years, would it be difficult for me to get a job? What kind of job would I have to take at first?
- If I had average ability, how much could I hope to earn during the first five years?
- What are the advantages and disadvantages of being an architect?
- If I were your son, would you advise me to become an architect?

5. Get over the mistaken belief that you are fitted for only a single occupation! Every normal person can succeed at a number of occupations, and every normal person would probably fail in many occupations. Take myself, for example: if I had studied and prepared myself for the following occupations, I believe I would have had a good chance of achieving some small measure of success and also of enjoying my work. I refer to such occupations as farming, fruit growing, scientific agriculture, medicine, selling, advertising, editing a country newspaper, teaching,

and forestry. On the other hand, I am sure I would have been unhappy, and a failure, at bookkeeping, accounting, engineering, operating a hotel or a factory, architecture, all mechanical trades, and hundreds of other activities.

.4.

Napoleon Hill

Think and Grow Rich

An international sensation in the personal development genre,
Think and Grow Rich *has sold tens of millions of copies ever*
since its publication in 1937. In this extract, the author shows
the importance of imagination and how creative thinking is key to
achieving great and lasting success in life and business.

~

IMAGINATION: THE WORKSHOP OF THE MIND

The imagination is literally the workshop wherein are fashioned
all plans created by man. The impulse, the DESIRE, is given
shape, form, and ACTION through the aid of the imaginative
faculty of the mind.

It has been said that man can create anything which he
can imagine. Of all the ages of civilization, this is the most
favourable for the development of the imagination, because
it is an age of rapid change. On every hand one may contact
stimuli which develop the imagination.

Through the aid of his imaginative faculty, man has
discovered, and harnessed, more of Nature's forces during the
past fifty years than during the entire history of the human
race, previous to that time. He has conquered the air so
completely, that the birds are a poor match for him in flying.
He has harnessed the ether, and made it serve as a means of
instantaneous communication with any part of the world. He

has analysed, and weighed the sun at a distance of millions of miles, and has determined, through the aid of IMAGINATION, the elements of which it consists. He has discovered that his own brain is both a broadcasting, and a receiving station for the vibration of thought, and he is beginning now to learn how to make practical use of this discovery. He has increased the speed of locomotion, until he may now travel at a speed of more than three hundred miles an hour.

The time will soon come when a man may breakfast in New York and lunch in San Francisco.

MAN'S ONLY LIMITATION, within reason, LIES IN HIS DEVELOPMENT AND USE OF HIS IMAGINATION. He has not yet reached the apex of development in the use of his imaginative faculty. He has merely discovered that he has an imagination, and has commenced to use it in a very elementary way.

Two Forms of Imagination

The imaginative faculty functions in two forms. One is known as 'synthetic imagination' and the other as 'creative imagination'.

Synthetic Imagination: through this faculty, one may arrange old concepts, ideas, or plans into new combinations. This faculty creates nothing. It merely works with the material of experience, education, and observation with which it is fed. It is the faculty used most by the inventor, with the exception of the who draws upon the creative imagination, when he cannot solve his problem through synthetic imagination.

Creative Imagination: through the faculty of creative imagination, the finite mind of man has direct communication with Infinite Intelligence. It is the faculty through which 'hunches' and 'inspirations' are received. It is by this faculty that all basic, or new ideas are handed over to man. It is through this faculty that thought vibrations from the minds of others are received. It is through this faculty that one individual may 'tune in', or communicate with the subconscious minds of other men.

The creative imagination works automatically, in the manner described in subsequent pages. This faculty functions ONLY when the conscious mind is vibrating at an exceedingly rapid rate, as for example, when the conscious mind is stimulated through the emotion of a strong desire.

The creative faculty becomes more alert, more receptive to vibrations from the sources mentioned, in proportion to its development through USE. This statement is significant! Ponder over it before passing on.

Keep in mind as you follow these principles, that the entire story of how one may convert DESIRE into money cannot be told in one statement. The story will be complete, only when one has MASTERED, ASSIMILATED, and BEGUN TO MAKE USE of all the principles.

The great leaders of business, industry, finance, and the great artists, musicians, poets, and writers became great, because they developed the faculty of creative imagination.

Both the synthetic and creative faculties of imagination become more alert with use, just as any muscle or organ of the body develops through use.

Desire is only a thought, an impulse. It is nebulous and ephemeral. It is abstract, and of no value, until it has been transformed into its physical counterpart. While the synthetic imagination is the one which will be used most frequently, in the process of transforming the impulse of DESIRE into money, you must keep in mind the fact, that you may face circumstances and situations which demand use of the creative imagination as well.

Your imaginative faculty may have become weak through inaction. It can be revived and made alert through USE. This faculty does not die, though it may become quiescent through lack of use. Center your attention, for the time being, on the development of the synthetic imagination, because this is the faculty which you will use more often in the process of converting desire into money.

Transformation of the intangible impulse, of DESIRE, into the tangible reality, of MONEY, calls for the use of a plan, or plans. These plans must be formed with the aid of the imagination, and mainly, with the synthetic faculty. Truly, thoughts are things, and their scope of operation is the world itself.

William George Jordan

The Majesty of Calmness: Individual Problems and Possibilities

*In his seminal work published in 1900, American essayist and editor
William George Jordan asks readers to reassess their approach to
life by viewing it through a simpler lens. This extract reveals the
close relationship between self-reliance and the actualization of true
potential, how believing in one's capabilities is the best way to turn
dreams into reality.*

~

THE DIGNITY OF SELF-RELIANCE

Self-confidence, without self-reliance, is as useless as a cooking
recipe—without food. Self-confidence sees the possibilities of
the individual; self-reliance realizes them. Self-confidence sees
the angel in the unhewn block of marble; self-reliance carves
it out for himself.

The man who is self-reliant says ever: 'No one can realize
my possibilities for me, but me; no one can make me good or
evil but myself.' He works out his own salvation—financially,
socially, mentally, physically, and morally. Life is an individual
problem that man must solve for himself. Nature accepts no
vicarious sacrifice, no vicarious service. Nature never recognizes
a proxy vote. She has nothing to do with middlemen—she deals
only with the individual. Nature is constantly seeking to show
man that he is his own best friend, or his own worst enemy.
Nature gives man the option on which he will be to himself.

All the athletic exercises in the world are of no value to the individual unless he compels those bars and dumbbells to yield to him, in strength and muscle, the power for which he, himself, pays in time and effort. He can never develop his muscles by sending his valet to a gymnasium.

The medicine chests of the world are powerless, in all the united efforts, to help the individual until he reach out and take for himself what is needed for his individual weakness.

All the religions of the world are but speculations in morals, mere theories of salvation, until the individual realizes that he must save himself by relying on the law of truth, as he sees it, and living his life in harmony with it, as fully as he can. But religion is not a Pullman car, with soft-cushioned seats, where he has but to pay for his ticket—and someone else does all the rest. In religion, as in all other great things, he is ever thrown back on his self-reliance. He should accept all helps, but—he must live his own life. He should not feel that he is a mere passenger; he is the engineer, and the train is his life. We must rely on ourselves, live our own lives, or we merely drift through existence—losing all that is best, all that is greatest, all that is divine.

All that others can do for us is to give us opportunity. We must ever be prepared for the opportunity when it comes, and to go after it and find it when it does not come, or that opportunity is to us—nothing. Life is but a succession of opportunities. They are for good or evil—as we make them.

Many of the alchemists of old felt that they lacked but one element; if they could obtain that one, they believed they could transmute the baser metals into pure gold. It is so in character. There are individuals with rare mental gifts, and delicate spiritual discernment who fail utterly in life because they lack the one element—self-reliance. This would unite all their energies, and focus them into strength and power.

The man who is not self-reliant is weak, hesitating and doubting in all he does. He fears to take a decisive step, because he dreads failure, because he is waiting for someone to advise him or because he dare not act in accordance with his own best judgment. In his cowardice and his conceit he sees all his non-success due to others. He is 'not appreciated', 'not recognized', he is 'kept down'. He feels that in some subtle way 'society is conspiring against him'. He grows almost vain as he thinks that no one has had such poverty, such sorrow, such affliction, such failure as have come to him.

The man who is self-reliant seeks ever to discover and conquer the weakness within him that keeps him from the attainment of what he holds dearest; he seeks within himself the power to battle against all outside influences. He realizes that all the greatest men in history, in every phase of human effort, have been those who have had to fight against the odds of sickness, suffering, sorrow. To him, defeat is no more than passing through a tunnel is to a traveller—he knows he must emerge again into the sunlight.

The nation that is strongest is the one that is most self-reliant, the one that contains within its boundaries all that its people need. If, with its ports all blockaded it has not within itself the necessities of life and the elements of its continual progress then—it is weak, held by the enemy, and it is but a question of time till it must surrender. Its independence is in proportion to its self-reliance, to its power to sustain itself from within. What is true of nations is true of individuals. The history of nations is but the biography of individuals magnified, intensified, multiplied, and projected on the screen of the past. History is the biography of a nation; biography is the history of an individual. So it must be that the individual who is most strong in any trial, sorrow, or need is he who can live from his inherent strength, who needs no scaffolding of commonplace sympathy to uphold him. He must ever be self-reliant.

The wealth and prosperity of ancient Rome, relying on her slaves to do the real work of the nation, proved the nation's downfall. The constant dependence on the captives of war to do the thousand details of life for them, killed self-reliance in the nation and in the individual. Then, through weakened self-reliance and the increased opportunity for idle, luxurious ease that came with it, Rome, a nation of fighters, became—a nation of men more effeminate than women. As we depend on others to do those things we should do for ourselves, our self-reliance weakens and our powers and our control of them becomes continuously less.

Man to be great must be self-reliant. Though he may not be so in all things, he must be self-reliant in the one in which he would be great. This self-reliance is not the self-sufficiency of conceit. It is daring to stand alone. Be an oak, not a vine. Be ready to give support, but do not crave it; do not be dependent on it. To develop your true self-reliance, you must see from the very beginning that life is a battle you must fight for yourself— you must be your own soldier. You cannot buy a substitute, you cannot win a reprieve, you can never be placed on the retired list. The retired list of life is—death. The world is busy with its own cares, sorrows and joys, and pays little heed to you. There is but one great password to success—self-reliance.

If you would learn to converse, put yourself into positions where you *must* speak. If you would conquer your morbidness, mingle with the bright people around you, no matter how difficult it may be. If you desire the power that someone else possesses, do not envy his strength, and dissipate your energy by weakly wishing his force were yours. Emulate the process by which it became his, depend on your self-reliance, pay the price for it, and equal power may be yours. The individual must look upon himself as an investment, of untold possibilities if rightly developed—a mine whose resources can never be known but by going down into it and bringing out what is hidden.

Man can develop his self-reliance by seeking constantly to surpass himself. We try too much to surpass others. If we seek ever to surpass ourselves, we are moving on a uniform line of progress, that gives a harmonious unifying to our growth in all its parts. Daniel Morrell, at one time president of the Cambria Rail Works that employed 7,000 men and made a rail famed throughout the world, was asked the secret of the great success of the works. 'We have no secret,' he said, 'but this—we always try to beat our last batch of rails.' Competition is good, but it has its danger side. There is a tendency to sacrifice real worth to mere appearance, to have seeming rather than reality. But the true competition is the competition of the individual with himself—his present seeking to excel his past. This means real growth from within. Self-reliance develops it, and it develops self-reliance. Let the individual feel thus as to his own progress and possibilities, and he can almost create his life as he will. Let him never fall down in despair at dangers and sorrows at a distance; they may be harmless, like Bunyan's stone lions, when he nears them.

The man who is self-reliant does not live in the shadow of someone else's greatness; he thinks for himself, depends on himself, and acts for himself. In throwing the individual thus back upon himself it is not shutting his eyes to the stimulus and light and new life that come with the warm pressure of the hand, the kindly word and the sincere expressions of true friendship. But true friendship is rare; its great value is in a crisis—like a lifeboat. Many a boasted friend has proved a leaking, worthless 'lifeboat' when the storm of adversity might make him useful. In these great crises of life, man is strong only as he is strong from within, and the more he depends on himself the stronger will he become, and the more able will he be to help others in the hour of their need. His very life will be a constant help and a strength to others, as he becomes to them a living lesson of the dignity of self-reliance.

.6.

Orison Swett Marden

Pushing to the Front

American author and founder of Success magazine,
Orison Swett Marden's writings on triumph in the
face of adversity have inspired millions, including stalwarts
like Theodore Roosevelt and Henry Ford. In this excerpt,
the author stresses on maximizing efficiency by cultivating
a strong hold on time and tapping into the hidden
potential of each day.

~

POSSIBILITIES IN SPARE MOMENTS

*Lost! Somewhere between sunrise and sunset,
two golden hours, each set with sixty diamond minutes.
No reward is offered, for they are gone forever.*

—Horace Mann

'What is the price of that book?' at length asked a man who had been dawdling for an hour in the front store of Benjamin Franklin's newspaper establishment. 'One dollar,' replied the clerk. 'One dollar,' echoed the lounger; 'can't you take less than that?' 'One dollar is the price,' was the answer.

The would-be purchaser looked over the books on sale a while longer, and then inquired: 'Is Mr Franklin in?'

'Yes,' said the clerk, 'he is very busy in the pressroom.'

'Well, I want to see him,' persisted the man.

The proprietor was called, and the stranger asked: 'What is the lowest, Mr Franklin, that you can take for that book?'

'One dollar and a quarter,' was the prompt rejoinder.

'One dollar and a quarter! Why, your clerk asked me only a dollar just now.'

'True,' said Franklin, 'and I could have better afforded to take a dollar than to leave my work.'

The man seemed surprised; but, wishing to end a parley of his own seeking, he demanded: 'Well, come now, tell me your lowest price for this book.'

'One dollar and a half,' replied Franklin.

'A dollar and a half! Why, you offered it yourself for a dollar and a quarter.'

'Yes,' said Franklin coolly, 'and I could better have taken that price then than a dollar and a half now.'

The man silently laid the money on the counter, took his book, and left the store, having received a salutary lesson from a master in the art of transmuting time, at will, into either wealth or wisdom.

Time-wasters are everywhere.

On the floor of the gold-working room, in the United States Mint at Philadelphia, there is a wooden latticework which is taken up when the floor is swept, and the fine particles of gold dust, thousands of dollars yearly, are thus saved. So every successful man has a kind of network to catch 'the raspings and parings of existence, those leavings of days and wee bits of hours' which most people sweep into the waste of life. He who hoards and turns to account all odd minutes, half hours, unexpected holidays, gaps 'between times,' and chasms of waiting for unpunctual persons, achieves results which astonish those who have not mastered this most valuable secret.

'All that I have accomplished, expect to, or hope to accomplish,' said Elihu Burritt, 'has been and will be by that plodding, patient, persevering process of accretion which builds the ant-heap—particle by particle, thought by thought, fact by fact. And if ever I was actuated by ambition, its highest and warmest aspiration reached no further than the hope to set before the young men of my country an example in employing those invaluable fragments of time called moments.'

'I have been wondering how Ned contrived to monopolize all the talents of the family,' said a brother, found in a brown study after listening to one of Burke's speeches in Parliament; 'but then I remember; when we were at play, he was always at work.'

The days come to us like friends in disguise, bringing priceless gifts from an unseen hand; but, if we do not use them, they are borne silently away, never to return. Each successive morning new gifts are brought, but if we fail to accept those that were brought yesterday and the day before, we become less and less able to turn them to account, until the ability to appreciate and utilize them is exhausted. Wisely was it said that lost wealth may be regained by industry and economy, lost knowledge by study, lost health by temperance and medicine, but lost time is gone forever.

'Oh, it's only five minutes or ten minutes till mealtime; there's no time to do anything now,' is one of the commonest expressions heard in the family. But what monuments have been built up by poor boys with no chance, out of broken fragments of time which many of us throw away! The very hours you have wasted, if improved, might have insured your success.

Marion Harland has accomplished wonders, and she has been able to do this by economizing the minutes to shape her novels and newspaper articles, when her children were in bed and whenever she could get a spare minute. Though she has done so much, yet all her life has been subject to interruptions which would have discouraged most women from attempting anything outside their regular family duties. She has glorified the commonplace as few other women have done. Harriet Beecher Stowe, too, wrote her great masterpiece, *Uncle Tom's Cabin*, in the midst of pressing household cares. Beecher read Froude's *England* a little each day while he had to wait for dinner. Longfellow translated the *Inferno* by snatches of ten minutes a day, while waiting for his coffee to boil, persisting for years until the work was done.

Oh, the power of ceaseless industry to perform miracles!

One hour a day withdrawn from frivolous pursuits and profitably employed would enable any man of ordinary capacity to master a complete science. One hour a day would in ten years make an ignorant man a well-informed man. It would earn enough to pay for two daily and two weekly papers, two leading magazines, and at least a dozen good books. In an hour a day a boy or girl could read twenty pages thoughtfully—over seven thousand pages, or eighteen large volumes in a year. An hour a day might make all the difference between bare existence and useful, happy living. An hour a day might make—nay, has made—an unknown man a famous one, a useless man a benefactor to his race. Consider, then, the mighty possibilities of two—four—yes, six hours a day that are, on the average, thrown away by young men and women in the restless desire for fun and diversion!

Great men have ever been misers of moments. Cicero said: 'What others give to public shows and entertainments, nay, even to mental and bodily rest, I give to the study of philosophy.' Lord Bacon's fame springs from the work of his leisure hours while Chancellor of England. During an interview with a great monarch, Goethe suddenly excused himself, went into an adjoining room and wrote down a thought for his *Faust*, lest it should be forgotten. Sir Humphry Davy achieved eminence in spare moments in an attic of an apothecary's shop. Pope would often rise in the night to write out thoughts that would not come during the busy day. Grote wrote his matchless *History of Greece* during the hours of leisure snatched from his duties as a banker.

No one is anxious about a young man while he is busy in useful work. But where does he eat his lunch at noon? Where does he go when he leaves his boarding-house at night? What does he do after supper? Where does he spend his Sundays and holidays? The way he uses his spare moments reveals his character. The great majority of youths who go to the bad are ruined after supper. Most of those who climb upward to honour and fame devote their evenings to study or work or the society of those who can help and improve them. Each evening is a crisis in the career of a young man. There is a deep significance in the lines of Whittier:

This day we fashion Destiny, our web of Fate we spin;
This day for all hereafter choose we holiness or sin.

Time is money. We should not be stingy or mean with it, but we should not throw away an hour any more than we would throw away a dollar-bill. Waste of time means waste of energy, waste of vitality, waste of character in dissipation. It means the waste of opportunities which will never come back. Beware how you kill time, for all your future lives in it.

'And it is left for each,' says Edward Everett, 'by the cultivation of every talent, by watching with an eagle's eye for every chance of improvement, by redeeming time, defying temptation, and scorning sensual pleasure, to make himself useful, honoured, and happy.'

.7.

Earl Prevette

How to Turn Your Ability into Cash

Pioneering American salesman Earl Prevette has written several inspirational tracts on business and sales, his most popular books being How to Turn Your Ability into Cash *and* How to Sell by Telephone. *In this essay, the author encourages the relentless pursuit of knowledge and having a firm grasp over one's areas of interest as the sure-footed way of making an unforgettable impression.*

~

JUST WHAT IS THE SOURCE OF POWER?

The Greeks have a word for it and it still remains the best answer after thousands of years.

Knowledge is power.

That phrase has been repeated so interminably over the centuries that today it is a cliché, which as you doubtless know, is a stereotyped expression for an obvious truth. But that does not detract from its value in the philosophy of life. We do not destroy a temple by flinging bricks through the window. When the violence abates, the temple stands.

The Greeks were right and so is the man who listens to their counsel.

I have discussed at length the high value of enthusiasm in any activity and I mean every word of it. But a few reservations are necessary. 'Do the thing and you shall have the power' is true. It is also true that power itself generates enthusiasm. I simply want to make the point that enthusiasm alone cannot take the place of power.

Let me put it another way. We think of a good salesman as a man who can talk. But the best salesman is the man who knows what he is talking about. That is power. Knowledge of the King's English is a great asset, but knowledge of your subject precedes it in importance. One helps the other, but the second comes first in impressing your audience. Know your stuff and the rest will follow. Enthusiasm carries contagion—it is catching. Power carries conviction—its message registers and its import remains.

So, we come to the secret of power, and the ancient Greeks and all human experience are in accord.

The secret is Knowledge.

How Knowledge Can Give You Power

Over the years I have met many successful men in all walks of life, and one thing has always impressed me. They were so saturated with their subject, whatever it happened to be, that usually it was the subject that did the talking rather than the speaker. The voice was the medium of expression, but you couldn't hear the voice for the story, so intense was the conviction behind it.

While lecturing on art on one occasion, in London, James McNeill Whistler, the celebrated American artist, was thus interrupted by one of his audience:

'But a minute ago, Mr Whistler, you were arguing.'

'I beg your pardon,' flashed Whistler, 'I am not arguing, I am telling you!'

Another authentic Whistler story is appropriate to this

chapter. In the case of Whistler v. Ruskin, growing out of Ruskin's scornful comment on Whistler's now famous 'Nocturne in Black and Gold,' for which he had asked two hundred guineas, Sir John Holker, Attorney General presiding, asked:

'How long did it take you to knock off that 'Nocturne'?'

'I beg your pardon,' said the witness.

Sir John apologized for his flippancy.

'About a day,' replied Whistler. 'I may have put a few touches to it on the following day.'

'And for two days' labour,' said Sir John, 'you ask two hundred guineas?'

'No,' answered Whistler, 'I ask it for the knowledge of a lifetime.'

The knowledge of a lifetime! Never was a more devastating answer to a more impudent question.

The Secret of Gaining Knowledge

But do not let the reference to a lifetime dampen your ardour for knowledge. A lifetime is life up to now, whether you are thirty, sixty, or ninety.

It is not years alone that constitute what we call experience, but the faith and struggle we crowd into them; and even experience in the treadmill sense of duration is not knowledge nor the way to knowledge.

Knowledge is the reward of those who bring more than a routine interest to a routine task; not merely picking up where someone left off, but seeking and finding ways and means by which the work can be more profitably continued. And we do not need to invoke top-flight instances such as Edison and Ford to prove that this passion for improvement and progress operates successfully in all walks and all stations of life. Here are a few cases that are known to me.

The private secretary to a brilliant but untutored man took his dictation and, in the finished scripts, corrected his English: then went on to make $150,000 a year as a writer. He had never written a line before, but he got the feeling that he could and went ahead and proved it. A ledger clerk in a small manufacturing concern, studying accounting at night, learned not only how to balance a set of books but how to spot the danger signal in a set of figures. Today he is an important financier. A salesman for household appliances, worn ragged by abortive calls on housewives, submitted some suggestions to the promotion department for improving his welcome and increasing his orders. Today he is vice-president in charge of sales. And the number of retail salespeople and stockroom employees who have graduated into buyers, executives, and even store owners is endless. More than forty years ago a young man employed in a popular New York department store quit, over the protests of his employers, and founded a congress of specialty shops on Fifth Avenue, which later became the most spectacular and successful operation of its kind in America. His name was Franklin Simon, and his achievement is still one of the great legends of modern merchandising. He set a pace that none could follow in his time and which few have equalled since.

The Secret of Advancement

How do they do it? How do people, in every industry, elevate themselves from subordinate positions to higher and continually higher appointments, without aid, without influence, without any help beyond their own endeavours? The answer, with few exceptions, is simple. They make an intense study of what they are doing and use it as a preparatory course for bettering the product, or the service, and themselves at the same time. The man who is absorbed in his present task to the exclusion of everything besides, is actually preoccupied with his own advancement. His job is his vehicle for pursuing that larger destiny that lies over the hill.

Whatever your orbit in life and whatever occupation you are engaged in, do not be satisfied to follow a pattern, but try to innovate and to improve the work of your predecessors. Seek knowledge, and the power you seek shall be added unto you.

Arthur Schopenhauer

Counsels and Maxims

One of the most influential German philosophers of the eighteenth century, Arthur Schopenhauer's philosophies have influenced the likes of Albert Einstein, Sigmund Freud, Leo Tolstoy, and Herman Hesse. This tract from his book advises against daydreaming and romanticizing struggles and difficulties as opposed to having an objective view of the situation.

~

IN ALL MATTERS AFFECTING OUR WEAL OR WOE, WE SHOULD BE...

careful not to let our imagination run away with us, and build no castles in the air. In the first place, they are expensive to build, because we have to pull them down again immediately, and that is a source of grief. We should be still more on our guard against distressing our hearts by depicting possible misfortunes. If these were misfortunes of a purely imaginary kind, or very remote and unlikely, we should at once see, on awaking from our dream, that the whole thing was mere illusion; we should rejoice all the more in a reality better than our dreams, or at most, be warned against misfortunes which, though very remote, were still possible. These, however, are not the sort of playthings in which imagination delights; it is only in idle hours that we build castles in the air, and they are always of a pleasing description. The matter which goes to form gloomy dreams are mischances which to some extent really threaten us, though it be from some distance; imagination makes us look larger and nearer and more terrible than they are in reality. This is a kind of dream which cannot be so readily shaken off on awaking as a pleasant one; for a pleasant dream is soon dispelled by reality, leaving, at most, a feeble hope lying in the lap of possibility. Once we have abandoned ourselves to a fit of the blues, visions are conjured up which do not so easily vanish again; for it is always just possible that the visions may be realized. But we are not always able to estimate the exact degree of possibility: possibility may easily pass into probability; and thus we deliver ourselves up to torture. Therefore we should be careful not to be over-anxious on any matter affecting our weal or our woe, not to carry our anxiety to unreasonable or injudicious limits; but coolly and dispassionately to deliberate upon the matter, as though it were an abstract question which did not touch us in particular. We should give no play to imagination here; for imagination is not judgment—it only conjures up visions, inducing an unprofitable and often very painful mood.

The rule on which I am here insisting should be most carefully observed towards evening. For as darkness makes us timid and apt to see terrifying shapes everywhere, there is something similar in the effect of indistinct thought; and uncertainty always brings with it a sense of danger. Hence, towards evening, when our powers of thought and judgment are relaxed—at the hour, as it were, of subjective darkness— the intellect becomes tired, easily confused, and unable to get at the bottom of things; and if, in that state, we meditate on matters of personal interest to ourselves, they soon assume a dangerous and terrifying aspect. This is mostly the case at night, when we are in bed; for then the mind is fully relaxed, and the power of judgment quite unequal to its duties; but imagination is still awake. Night gives a black look to everything, whatever it may be. This is why our thoughts, just before we go to sleep, or as we lie awake through the hours of the night, are usually such confusions and perversions of facts as dreams themselves; and when our thoughts at that time are concentrated upon our own concerns, they are generally as black and monstrous as possible. In the morning all such nightmares vanish like dreams: as the Spanish proverb has it, 'noche tinta, bianco el dia'—*the night is coloured, the day is white. But even towards nightfall, as soon as the candles are lit, the mind, like the eye, no longer sees things so clearly as by day: it is a time unsuited to serious meditation, especially on unpleasant subjects. The morning is the proper time for that—as indeed for all efforts without exception, whether mental or bodily. For the morning is the youth of the day, when everything is bright, fresh, and easy of attainment; we feel strong then, and all our faculties are completely at our disposal. Do not shorten the morning by getting up late, or waste it in unworthy occupations or in talk; look upon it as the quintessence of life, as to a certain extent sacred. Evening is like old age: we are languid, talkative, silly. Each day is a little life: every waking and rising a little birth, every fresh morning a little youth, every going to rest and sleep a little death.*

But condition of health, sleep, nourishment, temperature, weather, surroundings, and much else that is purely external, have, in general, an important influence upon our mood and therefore upon our thoughts. Hence both our view of any matter and our capacity for any work are very much subject to time and place. So it is best to profit by a good mood—for how seldom it comes!—

Nehmt die gute Stimmung wahr,
Denn sie kommt so selten.

We are not always able to form new ideas about our surroundings, or to command original thoughts, they come if they will, and when they will. And so, too, we cannot always succeed in completely considering some personal matter at the precise time at which we have determined beforehand to consider it, and just when we set ourselves to do so. For the peculiar train of thought which is favourable to it may suddenly become active without any special call being made upon it, and we may then follow it up with keen interest. In this way reflection, too, chooses its own time.

This reining in of the imagination which I am recommending, will also forbid us to summon up the memory of the past misfortune, to paint a dark picture of the injustice or harm that has been done to us, the losses we have sustained, the insults, slights, and annoyances to which we have been exposed: for to do that is to rouse into fresh life all those hateful passions long laid asleep—the anger and resentment which disturb and pollute our nature. In an excellent parable, Proclus, the Neoplatonist, points out how in every town the mob dwells side by side with those who are rich and distinguished: so, too, in every man, be he never so noble and dignified, there is, in the depth of his nature, a mob of low and vulgar desires which constitute him an animal. It will not do to let this mob revolt or even so much as peep forth from its hiding-place; it is hideous of mien, and its rebel leaders are those flights of imagination which I have been describing. The smallest annoyance, whether it comes from our fellow men or from the things around us, may swell up into a monster of dreadful aspect, putting us at our wits' end—and all because we go on brooding over our troubles and painting them in the most glaring colours and on the largest scale. It is much better to take a very calm and prosaic view of what is disagreeable; for that is the easiest way of bearing it.

If you hold small objects close to your eyes, you limit your field of vision and shut out the world. And, in the same way, the people or the things which stand nearest, even though they are of the very smallest consequence, are apt to claim an amount of attention much beyond their due, occupying us disagreeably, and leaving no room for serious thoughts and affairs of importance. We ought to work against this tendency.

.9.

Samuel Smiles

Character

Scottish author, government reformer, and political thinker Samuel Smiles was best known for his motivational works on individual effort, perseverance, and self-improvement. The following section, from his book Character, *highlights the significance of practical wisdom gained through experiences. While precepts and instructions are important, an open mind, hard work, and active engagement with the world will aid character development and add purpose to our existence.*

~

THE DISCIPLINE OF EXPERIENCE

Practical wisdom is only to be learnt in the school of experience. Precepts and instructions are useful so far as they go, but, without the discipline of real life, they remain of the nature of theory only. The hard facts of existence have to be faced, to give that touch of truth to character which can never be imparted by reading or tuition, but only by contact with the broad instincts of common men and women.

To be worth anything, character must be capable of standing firm upon its feet in the world of daily work, temptation, and trial; and able to bear the wear-and-tear of actual life. Cloistered virtues do not count for much. The life that rejoices in solitude may be only rejoicing in selfishness. Seclusion may indicate contempt for others; though more usually it means indolence, cowardice, or self-indulgence. To every human being belongs his fair share of manful toil and human duty; and it cannot be shirked without loss to the individual himself, as well as to the community to which he belongs. It is only by mixing in the daily life of the world, and taking part in its affairs, that practical knowledge can be acquired, and wisdom learnt. It is there that we find our chief sphere of duty, that we learn the discipline of work, and that we educate ourselves in that patience, diligence, and endurance which shape and consolidate the character. There, we encounter the difficulties, trials, and temptations which, according as we deal with them, give a colour to our entire after-life; and there, too, we become subject to the great discipline of suffering from which we learn far more than from the safe seclusion of the study or the cloister.

Contact with others is also requisite to enable a man to know himself. It is only by mixing freely in the world that one can form a proper estimate of his own capacity. Without such experience, one is apt to become conceited, puffed-up, and arrogant; at all events, he will remain ignorant of himself, though he may heretofore have enjoyed no other company.

Swift once said: 'It is an uncontroverted truth, that no man ever made an ill-figure who understood his own talents, nor a good one who mistook them.' Many persons, however, are readier to take measure of the capacity of others than of themselves. 'Bring him to me,' said a certain Dr Tronchin, of Geneva, speaking of Rousseau—'Bring him to me, that I may see whether he has got anything in him!'—the probability being that Rousseau, who knew himself better, was much more likely to take measure of Tronchin than Tronchin was to take measure of him.

A due amount of self-knowledge is, therefore, necessary for those who would BE anything or DO anything in the world.

It is also one of the first essentials to the formation of distinct personal convictions. Frederic Perthes once said to a young friend: 'You know only too well what you CAN do; but till you have learned what you CANNOT do, you will neither accomplish anything of moment, nor know inward peace.'

Anyone who would profit by experience will never be above asking for help. He who thinks himself already too wise to learn of others, will never succeed in doing anything either good or great. We have to keep our minds and hearts open, and never be ashamed to learn, with the assistance of those who are wiser and more experienced than ourselves.

The man made wise by experience endeavours to judge correctly of the thugs which come under his observation, and form the subject of his daily life. What we call common sense is, for the most part, but the result of common experience wisely improved. Nor is great ability necessary to acquire it, so much as patience, accuracy, and watchfulness. Hazlitt thought the most sensible people to be met with are intelligent men of business and of the world, who argue from what they see and know, instead of spinning cobweb distinctions of what things ought to be.

For the same reason, women often display more good sense than men, having fewer pretensions, and judging of things naturally, by the involuntary impression they make on the mind. Their intuitive powers are quicker, their perceptions more acute, their sympathies more lively, and their manners more adaptive to particular ends. Hence their greater tact as displayed in the management of others, women of apparently slender intellectual powers often contriving to control and regulate the conduct of men of even the most impracticable nature. Pope paid a high compliment to the tact and good sense of Mary, Queen of William III, when he described her as possessing, not a science, but (what was worth all else) prudence.

The whole of life may be regarded as a great school of experience, in which men and women are the pupils. As in a school, many of the lessons learnt there must needs be taken on trust. We may not understand them, and may possibly think it hard that we have to learn them, especially where the teachers are trials, sorrows, temptations, and difficulties; and yet we must not only accept their lessons, but recognize them as being divinely appointed.

To what extent have the pupils profited by their experience in the school of life? What advantage have they taken of their opportunities for learning? What have they gained in discipline of heart and mind?—how much in growth of wisdom, courage, self-control? Have they preserved their integrity amidst prosperity, and enjoyed life in temperance and moderation? Or, has life been with them a mere feast of selfishness, without care or thought for others? What have they learnt from trial and adversity? Have they learnt patience, submission, and trust in God?—or have they learnt nothing but impatience, querulousness, and discontent?

The results of experience are, of course, only to be achieved by living; and living is a question of time. The man of experience learns to rely upon Time as his helper. 'Time and I against any two,' was a maxim of Cardinal Mazarin. Time has been described as a beautifier and as a consoler; but it is also a teacher. It is the food of experience, the soil of wisdom. It may be the friend or the enemy of youth; and Time will sit beside the old as a consoler or as a tormentor, according as it has been used or misused, and the past life has been well or ill spent.

'Time,' says George Herbert, 'is the rider that breaks

youth.' To the young, how bright the new world looks!—how full of novelty, of enjoyment, of pleasure! But as years pass, we find the world to be a place of sorrow as well as of joy. As we proceed through life, many dark vistas open upon us—of toil, suffering, difficulty, perhaps misfortune and failure. Happy they who can pass through and amidst such trials with a firm mind and pure heart, encountering trials with cheerfulness, and standing erect beneath even the heaviest burden!

A little youthful ardour is a great help in life, and is useful as an energetic motive power. It is gradually cooled down by Time, no matter how glowing it has been, while it is trained and subdued by experience. But it is a healthy and hopeful indication of character—to be encouraged in a right direction, and not to be sneered down and repressed. It is a sign of a vigorous unselfish nature, as egotism is of a narrow and selfish one; and to begin life with egotism and self-sufficiency is fatal to all breadth and vigour of character. Life, in such a case, would be like a year in which there was no spring. Without a generous seedtime, there will be an unflowering summer and an unproductive harvest. And youth is the springtime of life, in which, if there be not a fair share of enthusiasm, little will be attempted, and still less done. It also considerably helps the working quality, inspiring confidence and hope, and carrying one through the dry details of business and duty with cheerfulness and joy.

There needs all the force that enthusiasm can give to enable a man to succeed in any great enterprise of life. Without it, the obstruction and difficulty he has to encounter on every side might compel him to succumb; but with courage and perseverance, inspired by enthusiasm, a man feels strong enough to face any danger, to grapple with any difficulty. What an enthusiasm was that of Columbus, who, believing in the existence of a new world, braved the dangers of unknown seas; and when those about him despaired and rose up against him, threatening to cast him into the sea, still stood firm upon his hope and courage until the great new world at length rose upon the horizon!

The brave man will not be baffled, but tries and tries again until he succeeds. The tree does not fall at the first stroke, but only by repeated strokes and after great labour. We may see the visible success at which a man has arrived, but forget the toil and suffering and peril through which it has been achieved. When a friend of Marshal Lefevre was complimenting him on his possessions and good fortune, the Marshal said: 'You envy me, do you? Well, you shall have these things at a better bargain than I had. Come into the court: I'll fire at you with a gun twenty times at thirty paces, and if I don't kill you, all shall be your own. What! you won't! Very well; recollect, then, that I have been shot at more than a thousand times, and much nearer, before I arrived at the state in which you now find me!'

The apprenticeship of difficulty is one which the greatest of men have had to serve. It is usually the best stimulus and discipline of character. It often evokes powers of action that, but for it, would have remained dormant. As comets are sometimes revealed by eclipses, so heroes are brought to light by sudden calamity. It seems as if, in certain cases, genius, like iron struck by the flint, needed the sharp and sudden blow of adversity to bring out the divine spark. There are natures which blossom and ripen amidst trials, which would only wither and decay in an atmosphere of ease and comfort.

Thus it is good for men to be roused into action and stiffened into self-reliance by difficulty, rather than to slumber away their lives in useless apathy and indolence. It is the struggle that is the condition of victory. If there were no difficulties, there would be no need of efforts; if there were no temptations, there would be no training in self-control, and but little merit in virtue; if there were no trial and suffering, there would be no education in patience and resignation. Thus difficulty, adversity, and suffering are not all evil, but often the best source of strength, discipline, and virtue.

And when we have done our work on earth—of necessity, of labour, of love, or of duty—like the silkworm that spins its little cocoon and dies, we too depart. But, short though our stay in life may be, it is the appointed sphere in which each has to work out the great aim and end of his being to the best of his power; and when that is done, the accidents of the flesh will affect but little the immortality we shall at last put on:

> *'Therefore we can go die as sleep, and trust*
> *Half that we have*
> *Unto an honest faithful grave;*
> *Making our pillows either down or dust!'*

10

Lucian B. Watkins

The Flower at My Window

Lucian Bottow Watkins (1879–1921) was an African-American poet born in Chesterfield, who fought in the First World War. In one of his most famous poems, The Flower at My Window, *he poignantly captures the delicate yet transient beauty of nature, comparing life's fleeting but precious moments to the powerful grace of a blooming flower.*

~

O! my heart now feels so cheerful as I go with
footsteps light
In the daily toil of my dear home;
And I'll tell to you the secret that now makes my life
so bright—
There's a flower at my window in full bloom.

It is radiant in the sunshine, and so cheerful after rain;
And it wafts upon the air its sweet perfume.
It is very, very lovely! May its beauties never wane—
This dear flower at my window in full bloom.

Nature has so clothed it in such glorious array,
And it does so cheer our home, and hearts illume;
Its dear mem'ry I will cherish though the flower fade
away—
This dear flower at my window in full bloom.

Oft I gaze upon this flower with its blossoms pure and
white.
And I think as I behold its gay costume,
While through life we all are passing may our lives be
always bright
Like this flower at my window in full bloom.

SECTION II

ACCUMULATING WEALTH

11

James Allen

Eight Pillars of Prosperity

A timeless classic by James Allen, the book explores the fundamental principles for achieving enduring success and abundance. In this lesson, the author shares insightful reflections on the importance of moral integrity and how dishonest practices weaken the foundation of any human endeavour.

~

EIGHT PILLARS

Prosperity rests upon a moral foundation. It is popularly supposed to rest upon an immoral foundation—that is, upon trickery, sharp practice, deception, and greed. One commonly hears even an otherwise intelligent man declare that 'No man can be successful in business unless he is dishonest,' thus regarding business prosperity—a good thing—as the effect of dishonesty—a bad thing. Such a statement is superficial and thoughtless, and reveals a total lack of knowledge of moral causation, as well as a very limited grasp of the facts of life. It is as though one should sow henbane and reap spinach, or erect a brick house on a quagmire—things impossible in the natural order of causation, and therefore not to be attempted. The spiritual or moral order of causation is not different in principle, but only in nature. The same law obtains in things unseen—in thoughts and deeds—as in things seen—in natural phenomena. Man sees the processes in natural objects, and acts in accordance with them, but not seeing the spiritual processes, he imagines that they do not obtain, and so he does not act in harmony with them.

Yet these spiritual processes are just as simple and just as sure as the natural processes. They are indeed the same natural modes manifesting in the world of mind. All the parables and a large number of the sayings of the Great Teachers are designed to illustrate this fact. The natural world is the mental world made visible. The seen is the mirror of the unseen. The upper half of a circle is in no way different from the lower half, but its sphericity is reversed. The material and the mental are not two detached arcs in the universe, they are the two halves of a complete circle. The natural and the spiritual are not at eternal enmity, but in the true order of the universe are eternally at one. It is in the unnatural—in the abuse of function and faculty— where division arises, and where main is wrested back, with repeated sufferings, from the perfect circle from which he has tried to depart. Every process in matter is also a process in mind. Every natural law has its spiritual counterpart.

Take any natural object, and you will find its fundamental processes in the mental sphere if you rightly search. Consider, for instance, the germination of a seed and its growth into a plant with the final development of a flower, and back to seed again. This also is a mental process. Thoughts are seeds which, falling in the soil of the mind, germinate and develop until they reach the completed stage, blossoming into deeds good or bad, brilliant or stupid, according to their nature, and ending as seeds of thought to be again sown in other minds. A teacher is a sower of seed, a spiritual agriculturist, while he who teaches himself is the wise farmer of his own mental plot. The growth of a thought is as the growth of a plant. The seed must be sown seasonably, and time is required for its full development into the plant of knowledge and the flower of wisdom.

While writing this, I pause, and turn to look through my study window, and there, a hundred yards away, is a tall tree in the top of which some enterprising rook from a rookery hard by, has, for the first time, built its nest. A strong, northeast wind is blowing, so that the top of the tree is swayed violently to and fro by the onset of the blast; yet there is no danger to that frail thing of sticks and hair, and the mother bird, sitting upon her eggs, has no fear of the storm. Why is this? It is because the bird has instinctively built her nest in harmony with principles which ensure the maximum strength and security.

A house or a temple built by man is a much more complicated structure than a bird's nest, yet it is erected in accordance with those mathematical principles that are everywhere evidenced in nature. And here is seen how man, in material things, obeys universal principles. He never attempts to put up a building in defiance of geometrical proportions, for he knows that such a building would be unsafe, and that the first storm would, in all probability, level it to the ground, if, indeed, it did not fall about his ears during the process of erection. Man in his material building scrupulously obeys the fixed principles of circle, square and angle, and, aided by rule, plumbline, and compasses, he raises a structure which will resist the fiercest storms, and afford him a secure shelter and safe protection.

Characters, like houses, only stand firmly when built on a foundation of moral law—and they are built up slowly and labouriously, deed by deed, for in the building of character, the bricks are deeds. Business and all human enterprises are not exempt from the eternal order, but can only stand securely by the observance of fixed laws. Prosperity, to be stable and enduring, must rest on a solid foundation of moral principle, and be supported by the adamantine pillars of sterling character and moral worth. In the attempt to run a business in defiance of moral principles, disaster, of one kind or another, is inevitable. The permanently prosperous men in any community are not its tricksters and deceivers, but its reliable and upright men.

Men speak of 'building up a business,' and, indeed, a business is as much a building as is a brick house or a stone church, albeit the process of building is a mental one. Prosperity, like a house, is a roof over a man's head, affording him protection and comfort. The roof of prosperity, then, is supported by the following eight pillars which are cemented in a foundation of moral consistency:

1. Energy
2. Economy
3. Integrity
4. System
5. Sympathy
6. Sincerity
7. Impartiality
8. Self-reliance

A business built up on the faultless practice of all these principles would be so firm and enduring as to be invincible. Nothing could injure it; nothing could undermine its prosperity, nothing could interrupt its success, or bring it to the ground; but that success would be assured with incessant increase so long as the principles were adhered to. On the other hand, where these principles were all absent, there could be no success of any kind; there could not even be a business at all, for there would be nothing to produce the adherence of one part with another; but there would be that lack of life, that absence of fibre and consistency which animates and gives body and form to anything whatsoever.

These eight principles, in greater or lesser degree, are the causative factors in all success of whatsoever kind. Underneath all prosperity they are the strong supports, and, howsoever appearances may be against such a conclusion, a measure of them informs and sustains every effort which is crowned with that excellence which men name success.

It is true that comparatively few successful men practice, in their entirety and perfection, all these eight principles, but there are those who do, and they are the leaders, teachers, and guides of men, the supports of human society, and the strong pioneers in the van of human evolution.

But while few achieve that moral perfection which ensures the acme of success, all lesser successes come from the partial observance of these principles which are so powerful in the production of good results that even perfection in any two or three of them alone is sufficient to ensure an ordinary degree of prosperity, and maintain a measure of local influence at least for a time, while the same perfection in two or three with partial excellence in all, or nearly all, the others, will render permanent that limited success and influence which will, necessarily, grow and extend in exact ratio with a more intimate knowledge and practice of those principles which, at present, are only partially incorporated in the character.

The boundary lines of a man's morality mark the limits of his success. So true is this that to know a man's moral status would be to know—to mathematically gauge—his ultimate success or failure. The temple of prosperity only stands in so far as it is supported by its moral pillars; as they are weakened, it becomes insecure; in so far as they are withdrawn, it crumbles away and totters to ruin.

.12.

Dale Carnegie

How to Stop Worrying and Start Living

Dale Carnegie's classic bestseller is one of the most widely-read self-help books in the world. In this excerpt, he offers practical advice on budgeting, avoiding pitfalls of increasing income without proper planning, and stresses on the need to be proactive in financial matters while maintaining a positive and realistic perspective.

~

HOW TO LESSON YOUR FINANCIAL WORRIES

If I knew how to solve everybody's financial worries, I wouldn't be writing this book, I would be sitting in the White House—right beside the president. But here is one thing I can do: I can quote some authorities on this subject and make some highly practical suggestions and point out where you can obtain books and pamphlets that will give you additional guidance.

A lot of readers are going to say: 'I wish this guy Carnegie had my bills to meet, my obligations to keep up on my weekly salary. If he did, I'll bet he would change his tune.' Well, I have had my financial troubles: I have worked ten hours a day at hard physical labour in the cornfields and hay barns of Missouri; worked until my one supreme wish was to be free from the aching pains of utter physical exhaustion. I was paid for that gruelling work not a dollar an hour, nor fifty cents, nor even ten cents. I was paid five cents an hour for a ten-hour day.

I know what it means to live for twenty years in houses without a bathroom or running water. I know what it means to sleep in bedrooms where the temperature is fifteen degrees below zero. I know what it means to walk miles to save a nickel car-fare and have holes in the bottom of my shoes and patches on the seat of my pants. I know what it means to order the cheapest dish on a restaurant menu, and to sleep with my trousers under the mattress because I couldn't afford to have them pressed by a tailor.

Yet, even during those times, I usually managed to save a few dimes and quarters out of my income because I was afraid not to. As a result of this experience, I realised that if you and I long to avoid debt and financial worries, then we have to do what a business firm does: we have to have a plan for spending our money and spend according to that plan. It is literally 'your business' what you do with your money. But what are the principles of managing our money? How do we begin to make a budget and a plan? Here are ten rules.

Rule No. 1: get the facts down on paper.

When Arnold Bennett started out in London fifty years ago to be a novelist, he was poor and hard-pressed. So he kept a record of what he did with every sixpence. Did he wonder where his money was going? No. He knew. He liked the idea so much that he continued to keep such a record even after he became rich, world-famous, and had a private yacht. John D. Rockefeller, Sr., also kept a ledger. He knew to the penny just where he stood before he said his prayers at night and climbed into bed. You and I, too, will have to get notebooks and start keeping records. For the rest of our lives? No, not necessarily. Experts on budgets recommend that we keep an accurate account of every nickel we spend for at least the first month-and, if possible, for three months. This is to give us an accurate record of where our money goes, so we can draw up a budget.

Oh, you know where your money goes? Well, maybe so; but if you do, you are one in a thousand!

Rule No. 2: get a tailor-made budget that really fits your needs.

The idea of a budget is not to wring all the joy out of life. The idea is to give us a sense of material security—which in many cases means emotional security and freedom from worry.

But how do you go about it? First, as I said, you must list all expenses. Then get advice. In many cities of twenty thousand and up, you will find family-welfare societies that will gladly give you free advice on financial problems and help you draw up a budget to fit your income.

Rule No. 3: learn how to spend wisely.

By this I mean: learn how to get the best value for your money. All large corporations have professional buyers and purchasing agents who do nothing but get the very best buys for their firms. As steward and manager of your personal estate, why shouldn't you do likewise?

Rule No. 4: don't increase your headaches with your income.

Mrs Elise Stapleton, a woman who spent years as a financial adviser told me that the budgets she dreads most to be called into consultation on are family incomes of five thousand dollars a year. I asked her why. 'Because,' she said, 'five thousand a year seems to be a goal to most American families. They may go along sensibly and sanely for years—then, when their income rises to five thousand a year, they think they have 'arrived'. They start branching out. Buy a house in the suburbs, 'that doesn't cost any more than renting an apartment'. Buy a car, a lot of new furniture, and a lot of new clothes, and the first thing you know, they are running into the red.

They are actually less happy than they were before because they have bitten off too much with their increase in income.'

That is only natural. We all want to get more out of life. But in the long run, which is going to bring us more happiness, forcing ourselves to live within a tight budget, or having dunning letters in the mail and creditors pounding on the front door?

Rule No. 5: try to build credit, in the event you must borrow.

If you are faced with an emergency and find you must borrow, life-insurance policies, Defence Bonds and Savings Certificates are literally money in your pocket. However, be sure your insurance policies have a savings aspect, if you want to borrow on them, for this means a cash value. Certain types of insurance, called 'term insurance', are merely for your protection over a given period of time and do not build up reserves. These policies are obviously of no use to you for borrowing purposes.

Therefore, the rule is: ask questions! Before you sign for a policy, find out if it has a cash value in case you have to raise money.

Rule No. 6: protect yourself against illness, fire, and emergency expenses.

Insurance is available, for relatively small sums, on all kinds of accidents, misfortunes, and conceivable emergencies. I am not suggesting that you cover yourself for everything from slipping in the bathtub to catching German measles—but I do suggest that you protect yourself against the major misfortunes that you know could cost you money and therefore do cost you worry. It's cheap at the price.

For example, I know a woman who had to spend ten days in a hospital last year and, when she came out, was presented a bill for exactly eight dollars! The answer? She had hospital insurance.

Rule No. 7: teach your children a responsible attitude toward money.

I shall never forget an idea I once read in *Your Life* magazine. The author, Stella Weston Turtle, described how she was teaching her little girl a sense of responsibility about money. She got an extra chequebook from the bank and gave it to her nine-year-old daughter. When the daughter was given her weekly allowance, she 'deposited' the money with her mother, who served as a bank for the child's funds. Then, throughout the week, whenever she wanted a cent or two, she 'drew a cheque' for that amount and kept track of her balance. The little girl not only found that fun, but began to learn real responsibility in handling her money. This is an excellent method and if you have a son or daughter of school age, and you want this child to learn how to handle money, I recommend it for your consideration.

Rule No. 8: if necessary, make a little extra money off your kitchen stove.

If after you budget your expenses wisely you still find that you don't have enough to make ends meet, you can then do one of two things: you can either scold, fret, worry, and complain, or you can plan to make a little additional money on the side. How? Well, all you have to do to make money is to fill an urgent need that isn't being adequately filled now. That is what Mrs Nellie Speer, 37-09 83rd Street, Jackson Heights, New York, did. In 1932, she found herself living alone in a three-room apartment.

Her husband had died, and both of her children were married. One day, while having some ice-cream at a drugstore soda fountain, she noticed that the fountain was also selling bakery pies that looked sad and dreary. She asked the proprietor if he would buy some real home-made pies from her. He ordered two. 'Although I was a good cook,' Mrs Speer said, as she told me the story, 'I had always had servants when we lived in Georgia, and I had never baked more than a dozen pies in my life. After getting that order for two pies, I asked a neighbour woman how to cook an apple-pie. The soda fountain customers were delighted with my first two home-baked pies, one apple, one lemon. The drugstore ordered five the next day. Then orders gradually came in from other fountains and luncheonettes. Within two years, I was baking five thousand pies a year—I was doing all the work myself in my own tiny kitchen, and I was making a thousand dollars a year clear, without a penny's expense except the ingredients that went into the pies.'

The demand for Mrs Speer's home-baked pastry became so great that she had to move out of her kitchen into a shop and hire two girls to bake for her: pies, cakes, bread, and rolls. During the war, people stood in line for an hour at a time to buy her home-baked foods.

'I have never been happier in my life,' Mrs Speer said. 'I work in the shop twelve to fourteen hours a day, but I don't get tired because it isn't work to me. It is an adventure in living. I am doing my part to make people a little happier. I am too busy to be lonesome or worried. My work has filled a gap in my life left vacant by the passing of my mother and husband and my home.'

Look around you. You will find many needs that are not filled. For example, if you train yourself to be a good cook, you can probably make money by starting cooking classes in your own kitchen. You can get your students by ringing door-bells.

Rule No. 9: don't gamble—ever

I am always astounded by the people who hope to make money by betting on the ponies or playing slot machines. I know a man who makes his living by owning a string of these 'one armed bandits', and he has nothing but contempt for the foolish people who are so naive as to imagine that they can beat a machine that is already rigged against them.

If we are determined to gamble, let's at least be smart. Let's find out what the odds are against us. How? By reading a book entitled authority on bridge and poker, a top-ranking mathematician, a professional statistician, and an insurance actuary. This book devotes five pages to telling you what the odds are against your winning when you play the ponies, roulette, craps, slot machines, draw poker, stud poker, contract bridge, auction pinochle, the stock market. This book also gives you the scientific, mathematical chances on a score of other activities. It doesn't pretend to show how to make money gambling. The author has no axe to grind. He merely shows you what the odds are against your winning in all the usual ways of gambling; and when you see the odds, you will pity the poor suckers who stake their hard-earned wages on horse races or cards or dice or slot machines. If you are tempted to shoot craps or play poker or bet on horses, this book may save you a hundred times—yes, maybe a thousand times—what it costs.

Rule No. 10: if we can't possibly improve our financial situation, let's be good to ourselves and stop resenting what can't be changed.

If we can't possibly improve our financial situation, maybe we can improve our mental attitude towards it. Let's remember that other people have their financial worries, too. We may be worried because we can't keep up with the Joneses; but the Joneses are probably worried because they can't keep up with the Ritzes; and the Ritzes are worried because they can't keep up with the Vanderbilts.

Some of the most famous men in American history have had their financial troubles. Both Lincoln and Washington had to borrow money to make the trip to be inaugurated as president.

If we can't have all we want, let's not poison our days and sour our dispositions with worry and resentment. Let's be good to ourselves. Let's try to be philosophical about it. 'If you have what seems to you insufficient,' said one of Rome's greatest philosophers, Seneca, 'then you will be miserable even if you possess the world.'

.13.

George Clason

The Richest Man in Babylon

A landmark book in the self-improvement genre, The Richest Man
in Babylon *by American author and businessman George Clason
imparts timeless financial wisdom through a collection of parables
set in ancient Babylon. In this section, he shares key principles
of wealth-building, such as saving, investing, and wise money
management, making it a perennial favourite for those seeking
financial success.*

~

SEVEN CURES TO A LEAN PURSE

When the Good King, Sargon, returned to Babylon after
defeating his enemies, the Elamites, he was confronted with
a serious situation. The Royal Chancellor explained it to the
King thus:

'After many years of great prosperity brought to our
people because your majesty built the great irrigation canals
and the mighty temples of the Gods, now that these works
are completed the people seem unable to support themselves.

'The labourers are without employment. The merchants
have few customers. The farmers are unable to sell their
produce. The people have not enough gold to buy food.'

'But where has all the gold gone that we spent for these
great improvements?' demanded the King.

'It has found its way, I fear,' responded the Chancellor,

'into the possession of a few very rich men of our city. It filtered through the fingers of most our people as quickly as the goat's milk goes through the strainer. Now that the stream of gold has ceased to flow, most of our people have nothing to for their earnings.'

The King was thoughtful for some time. Then he asked, 'Why should so few men be able to acquire all the gold?'

'Because they know how,' replied the Chancellor. 'One may not condemn a man for succeeding because he knows how. Neither may one with justice take away from a man what he has fairly earned, to give to men of less ability.'

'But why,' demanded the King, 'should not all the people learn how to accumulate gold and therefore become themselves rich and prosperous?

'Quite possible, your excellency. But who can teach them? Certainly not the priests, because they know naught of money making.'

'Who knows best in all our city how to become wealthy, Chancellor?' asked the King.

'Thy question answers itself, your majesty. Who has amassed the greatest wealth, in Babylon?'

'Well said, my able Chancellor. It is Arkad. He is richest man in Babylon. Bring him before me on the morrow.'

Upon the following day, as the King had decreed, Arkad appeared before him, straight and sprightly despite his three score years and ten.

'Arkad,' spoke the King, 'is it true thou art the richest man in Babylon?'

'So it is reported, your majesty, and no man disputes it.'

'How becamest thou so wealthy?'

'By taking advantage of opportunities available to all citizens of our good city.'

'Thou hadst nothing to start with?'

'Only a great desire for wealth. Besides this, nothing.'

'Arkad,' continued the King, 'our city is in a very unhappy state because a few men know how to acquire wealth and therefore monopolize it, while the mass of our citizens lack the knowledge of how to keep any part of the gold they receive.

'It is my desire that Babylon be the wealthiest city in the world. Therefore, it must be a city of many wealthy men. Therefore, we must teach all the people how to acquire riches. Tell me, Arkad, is there any secret to acquiring wealth? Can it be taught?'

'It is practical, your majesty. That which one man knows can be taught to others.'

The king's eyes glowed. 'Arkad, thou speaketh the words I wish to hear. Wilt thou lend thyself to this great cause? Wilt thou teach thy knowledge to a school for teachers, each of whom shall teach others until there are enough trained to teach these truths to every worthy subject in my domain?'

Arkad bowed and said, 'I am thy humble servant to command. Whatever knowledge I possess will I gladly give for the betterment of my fellowmen and the glory of my King. Let your good chancellor arrange for me a class of one hundred men and I will teach to them those seven cures which did fatten my purse, than which there was none leaner in all Babylon.'

A fortnight later, in compliance with the King's command, the chosen hundred assembled in the great hall of the Temple of Learning, seated upon colourful rings in a semicircle. Arkad sat beside a small taboret upon which smoked a sacred lamp sending forth a strange and pleasing odor.

'Behold the richest man in Babylon,' whispered a student, nudging his neighbour as Arkad arose. 'He is but a man even as the rest of us.'

'As a dutiful subject of our great King,' Arkad began, 'I stand before you in his service. Because once I was a poor youth who did greatly desire gold, and because I found knowledge that enabled me to acquire it, he asks that I impart unto you my knowledge.

'I started my fortune in the humblest way. I had no advantage not enjoyed as fully by you and every citizen in Babylon.

'The first storehouse of my treasure was a well-purse. I loathed its useless emptiness. I desired it be round and full, clinking with the sound of gold. Therefore, I sought every remedy for a lean purse. I found seven.

'To you, who are assembled before me, shall I explain the seven cures for a lean purse which I do recommend to all men who desire much gold. Each day for seven days will I explain to you one of the seven remedies.

'Listen attentively to the knowledge that I will impart. Debate it with me. Discuss it among yourselves. Learn these lessons thoroughly, that ye may also plant in your own purse the seed of wealth. First must each of you start wisely to build a fortune of his own. Then wilt thou be competent, and only then, to teach these truths to others.

'I shall teach to you in simple ways how to fatten your purses. This is the first step leading to the temple of wealth, and no man may climb who cannot plant his feet firmly upon the first step. 'We shall now consider the first cure.'

THE FIRST CURE
Start thy purse to fattening

Arkad addressed a thoughtful man in the second row. 'My good friend, at what craft workest thou?'

'I,' replied the man, 'am a scribe and carve records upon the clay tablets.'

'Even at such labour did I myself earn my first coppers. Therefore, thou hast the same opportunity to build a fortune.'

He spoke to a florid-faced man, farther back. 'Pray tell also what dost thou to earn thy bread?'

'I,' responded this man, 'am a meat butcher. I do buy the goats the farmers raise and kill them and sell the meat to the housewives and the hides to the sandal makers.'

'Because thou dost also labour and earn, thou hast every advantage to succeed that I did possess.'

In this way did Arkad proceed to find out how each man laboured to earn his living. When he had done questioning them, he said:

'Now, my students, ye can see that there are many trades and labours at which men may earn coins. Each of the ways of earning is a stream of gold from which the worker doth divert by his labours a portion to his own purse. Therefore into the purse of each of you flows a stream of coins large or small according to his ability. Is it not so?'

Thereupon they agreed that it was so.

'Then,' continued Arkad, 'if each of you desireth to build for himself a fortune, is it not wise to start by utilizing that source of wealth which he already has established?'

To this they agreed.

Then Arkad turned to a humble man who had declared himself an egg merchant. 'If thou select one of thy baskets and put into it each morning ten eggs and take out from it each evening nine eggs, what will eventually happen?'

'It will become in time overflowing.'

'Why?'

'Because each day I put in one more egg than I take out.'

Arkad turned to the class with a smile. 'Does any man here have a lean purse?'

First they looked amused. Then they laughed. Lastly they waved their purses in jest.

'All right,' he continued, 'Now I shall tell thee the first remedy I learned to cure a lean purse. Do exactly as I have suggested to the egg merchant. *For every ten coins thou placest within thy purse take out for use but nine. Thy purse will start to fatten at once and its increasing weight will feel good in thy hand and bring satisfaction to thy soul.*

'Deride not what I say because of its simplicity. Truth is always simple. I told thee I would tell how built my fortune. This was my beginning. I, too, carried a lean purse and cursed it because there was naught within to satisfy my desires. But when I began to take out from my purse but nine parts of ten I put in, it began to fatten. So will thine.

'Now I will tell a strange truth, the reason for which I know not. When I ceased to pay out more than nine-tenths of my earnings, I managed to get along just as well. I was not shorter than before. Also, ere long, did coins come to me more easily than before. Surely it is a law of the Gods that unto him who keepeth and spendeth not a certain part of all his earnings, shall gold come more easily. Likewise, him whose purse is empty does gold avoid.

'Which desirest thou the most? Is it the gratification of thy desires of each day, a jewel, a bit of finery, better raiment, more food; things quickly gone and forgotten? Or is it substantial belongings, gold, lands, herds, merchandise, income-bringing investments? The coins thou takest from thy purse bring the first. The coins thou leavest within it will bring the latter.

'This, my students, was the first cure I did discover for my lean purse: 'For each ten coins I put in, to spend but nine.'

Debate this amongst yourselves. If any man proves it untrue, tell me upon the morrow when we shall meet again.'

THE SECOND CURE
Control thy expenditures

'Some of your members, my students, have asked me this: How can a man keep one-tenth of all he earns in his purse when all the coins he earns are not enough for his necessary expenses?' So did Arkad address his students upon the second day.

'Yesterday how many of thee carried lean purses?'

'All of us,' answered the class.

'Yet, thou do not all earn the same. Some earn much more than others. Some have much larger families to support. Yet, all purses were equally lean. Now I will tell thee an unusual truth about men and sons of men. It is this; That what each of us calls our 'necessary expenses' will always grow to equal our incomes unless we protest to the contrary.

'Confuse not the necessary expenses with thy desires. Each of you, together with your good families, have more desires than your earnings can gratify. Therefore are thy earnings spent to gratify these desires insofar as they will go. Still thou retainest many ungratified desires.

'All men are burdened with more desires than they can gratify. Because of my wealth thinkest thou I may gratify every desire? 'Tis a false idea. There are limits to my time. There are limits to my strength. There are limits to the distance I may travel. There are limits to what I may eat. There are limits to the zest with which I may enjoy.

'I say to you that just as weeds grow in a field wherever the farmer leaves space for their roots, even so freely do desires grow in men whenever there is a possibility of their being gratified. Thy desires are a multitude and those that thou mayest gratify are but few.

'Study thoughtfully thy accustomed habits of living. Herein may be most often found certain accepted expenses that may wisely be reduced or eliminated. Let thy motto be one hundred percent of appreciated value demanded for each coin spent.

'Therefore, engrave upon the clay each thing for which thou desireth to spend. Select those that are necessary and others that are possible through the expenditure of nine-tenths of thy income. Cross out the rest and consider them but a part of that great multitude of desires that must go unsatisfied and regret them not.

'Budget then thy necessary expenses. Touch not the one-tenth that is fattening thy purse. Let this be thy great desire that is being fulfilled. Keep working with thy budget, keep adjusting it to help thee. Make it thy first assistant in defending thy fattening purse.'

Hereupon one of the students, wearing a robe of red and gold, arose and said, 'I am a free man. I believe that it is my right to enjoy the good things of life. Therefore do I rebel against the slavery of a budget which determines just how much I may spend and for what. I feel it would take much pleasure from my life and make me little more than a pack-ass to carry a burden.'

To him Arkad replied, 'Who, my friend, would determine thy budget?'

'I would make it for myself,' responded the protesting one.

'In that case were a pack-ass to budget his burden would he include therein jewels and rugs and heavy bars of gold? Not so. He would include hay and grain and a bag of water for the desert trail.

'The purpose of a budget is to help thy purse to fatten.

It is to assist thee to have thy necessities and, insofar as attainable, thy other desires. It is to enable thee to realize thy most cherished desires by defending them from thy casual wishes. Like a bright light in a dark cave thy budget shows up the leaks from thy purse and enables thee to stop them and control thy expenditures for definite and gratifying purposes.

'This, then, is the second cure for a lean purse. Budget thy expenses that thou mayest have coins to pay for thy necessities, to pay for thy enjoyments and to gratify thy worthwhile desires without spending more than nine-tenths of thy earnings.'

THE THIRD CURE
Make thy gold multiply

'Behold thy lean purse is fattening. Thou hast disciplined thyself to leave therein one-tenth of all thou earneth. Thou hast controlled thy expenditures to protect thy growing treasure. Next, we will consider means to put thy treasure to labour and to increase. Gold in a purse is gratifying to own and satisfieth a miserly soul but earns nothing. The gold we may retain from our earnings is but the start. The earnings it will make shall build our fortunes.' So spoke Arkad upon the third day to his class.

'How therefore may we put our gold to work? My first investment was unfortunate, for I lost all. Its tale I will relate later. My first profitable investment was a loan I made to a man named Aggar, a shield maker. Once each year did he buy large shipments of bronze brought from across the sea to use in his trade. Lacking sufficient capital to pay the merchants, he would borrow from those who had extra coins. He was an honourable man. His borrowing he would repay, together with a liberal rental, as he sold his shields.

'Each time I loaned to him I loaned back also the rental he had paid to me. Therefore not only did my capital increase, but its earnings likewise increased.

Most gratifying was it to have these sums return to my purse. 'I tell you, my students, a man's wealth is not in the coins he carries in his purse; it is the income he buildeth, the golden stream that continually floweth into his purse and keepeth it always bulging. That is what every man desireth. That is what thou, each one of thee desireth; an income that continueth to come whether thou work or travel.

'Great income I have acquired. So great that I am called a very rich man. My loans to Aggar were my first training in profitable investment. Gaining wisdom from this experience, I extended my loans and investments as my capital increased. From a few sources at first, from many sources later, flowed into my purse a golden stream of wealth available for such wise uses as I should decide.

'Behold, from my humble earnings I had begotten a hoard of golden slaves, each labouring and earning more gold. As they laboured for me, so their children also laboured and their children's children until great was the income from their combined efforts.

'Gold increaseth rapidly when making reasonable earnings as thou wilt see from the following: A farmer, when his first son was born, took ten pieces of silver to a moneylender and asked him to keep it on rental for his son until he became twenty years of age. This the moneylender did, and agreed the rental should be one-fourth of its value each four years. The farmer asked, because this sum he had set aside as belonging to his son, that the rental be add to the principal.

'When the boy had reached the age of twenty years, the farmer again went to the moneylender to inquire about the silver. The moneylender explained that because this sum had been increased by compound interest, the original ten pieces of silver had now grown to thirty and one-half pieces.

'The farmer was well pleased and because the son did not need the coins, he left them with the moneylender. When the son became fifty years of age, the father meantime having passed to the other world, the moneylender paid the son in settlement one hundred and sixty-seven pieces of silver.

'Thus in fifty years had the investment multiplied itself at rental almost seventeen times.

'This, then, is the third cure for a lean purse: *to put each coin to labouring that it may reproduce its kind even as the flocks of the field and help bring to thee income, a stream of wealth that shall flow constantly into thy purse.*'

THE FOURTH CURE
Guard thy treasures from loss

'Misfortune loves a shining mark. Gold in a man's purse must be guarded with firmness, else it be lost. Thus it is wise that we must first secure small amounts and learn to protect them before the Gods entrust us with larger.' So spoke Arkad upon the fourth day to his class.

'Every owner of gold is tempted by opportunities whereby it would seem that he could make large sums by its investment in most plausible projects. Often friends and relatives are eagerly entering such investment and urge him to follow.

'The first sound principle of investment is security for thy principal. Is it wise to be intrigued by larger earnings when thy principal may be lost? I say not. The penalty of risk is probable loss. Study carefully, before parting with thy treasure, each assurance that it may be safely reclaimed. Be not misled by thine own romantic desires to make wealth rapidly.

'Before thou loan it to any man assure thyself of his ability to repay and his reputation for doing so, that thou mayest not unwittingly be making him a present of thy hard-earned treasure. Before thou entrust it as an investment in any field acquaint thyself with the dangers which may beset it.

'My own first investment was a tragedy to me at the time. The guarded savings of a year I did entrust to a brickmaker, named Azmur, who was travelling over the far seas and in Tyre agreed to buy for me the rare jewels of the Phoenicians. These we would sell upon his return and divide the profits. The Phoenicians were scoundrels and sold him bits of glass. My treasure was lost. Today, my training would show to me at once the folly of entrusting a brickmaker to buy jewels.

'Therefore, do I advise thee from the wisdom of my experiences: be not too confident of thine own wisdom in entrusting thy treasures to the possible pitfalls of investments. Better by far to consult the wisdom of those experienced in handling money for profit. Such advice is freely given for the asking and may readily possess a value equal in gold to the sum thou considerest investing. In truth, such is its actual value if it save thee from loss.

'This, then, is the fourth cure for a lean purse, and of great importance if it prevent thy purse from being emptied once it has become well filled. *Guard thy treasure from loss by investing only where thy principal is safe, where it may be reclaimed if desirable, and where thou will not fail to collect a fair rental. Consult with wise men. Secure the advice of those experienced in the profitable handling of gold. Let their wisdom protect thy treasure from unsafe investments.'*

THE FIFTH CURE
Make of thy dwelling a profitable investment

'If a man setteth aside nine parts of his earnings upon which to live and enjoy life, and if any part of this nine parts he can turn into a profitable investment without detriment to his wellbeing, then so much faster will his treasures grow.' So spake Arkad to his class at their fifth lesson.

'All too many of our men of Babylon do raise their families in unseemly quarters. They do pay to exacting landlords liberal rentals for rooms where their wives have not a spot to raise the blooms that gladden a woman's heart and their children have no place to play their games except in the unclean alleys.

'No man's family can fully enjoy life unless they do have a plot of ground wherein children can play in the clean earth and where the wife may raise not only blossoms but good rich herbs to feed her family.

'To a man's heart it brings gladness to eat the figs from his own trees and the grapes of his own vines. To own his own domicile and to have it a place he is proud to care for, putteth confidence in his heart and greater effort behind all his endeavours. Therefore, do I recommend that every man own the roof that sheltereth him and his.

'Nor is it beyond the ability of any well intentioned man to own his home. Hath not our great king so widely extended the walls of Babylon that within them much land is now unused and may be purchased at sums most reasonable?

'Also I say to you, my students, that the moneylenders gladly consider the desires of men who seek homes and land for their families. Readily may thou borrow to pay the brickmaker and the builder for such commendable purposes, if thou can show a reasonable portion of the necessary sum which thou thyself hath provided for the purpose.

'Then when the house be built, thou canst pay the moneylender with the same regularity as thou didst pay the landlord. Because each payment will reduce thy indebtedness to the moneylender, a few years will satisfy his loan.

'Then will thy heart be glad because thou wilt own in thy own right a valuable property and thy only cost will be the king's taxes.

'Also wilt thy good wife go more often to the river to wash thy robes, that each time returning she may bring a goatskin of water to pour upon the growing things.

'Thus come many blessings to the man who owneth his own house. And greatly will it reduce his cost of living, making available more of his earnings for pleasures and the gratification of his desires. This, then, is the fifth cure for a lean purse: *own thy own home.*'

THE SIXTH CURE
Insure a future income

'The life of every man proceedeth from his childhood to his old age. This is the path of life and no man may deviate from it unless the Gods call him prematurely to the world beyond. Therefore do I say that it behooves a man to make preparation for a suitable income in the days to come, when he is no longer young, and to make preparations for his family should he be no longer with them to comfort and support them. This lesson shall instruct thee in providing a full purse when time has made thee less able to learn.' So Arkad addressed his class upon the sixth day.

'The man who, because of his understanding of the laws of wealth, acquireth a growing surplus, should give thought to those future days. He should plan certain investments or provision that may endure safely for many years, yet will be available when the time arrives which he has so wisely anticipated.

'There are diverse ways by which a man may provide with safety for his future. He may provide a hiding place and there bury a secret treasure. Yet, no matter with what skill it be hidden, it may nevertheless become the loot of thieves. For this reason I recommend not this plan.

'A man may buy houses or lands for this purpose. If wisely chosen as to their usefulness and value in the future, they are permanent in their value and their earnings or their sale will provide well for his purpose.

'A man may loan a small sum to the moneylender and increase it at regular periods. The rental which the moneylender adds to this will largely add to its increase. I do know a sandal maker, named Ansan, who explained to me not long ago that each week for eight years he had deposited with his moneylender two pieces of silver. The moneylender had but recently given him an accounting over which he greatly rejoiced. The total of his small deposits with their rental at the customary rate of one-fourth their value for each four years, had now become a thousand and forty pieces of silver.

'I did gladly encourage him further by demonstrating to him with my knowledge of the numbers that in twelve years more, if he would keep his regular deposits of but two pieces of silver each week, the moneylender would then owe him four thousand pieces of silver, a worthy competence for the rest of his life.

'Surely, when such a small payment made with regularity doth produce such profitable results, *no man can afford not to insure a treasure for his old age and the protection of his family, no matter how prosperous his business and his investments may be.*

'I would that I might say more about this. In my mind rests a belief that someday wise thinking men will devise a plan to insure against death whereby many men pay in but a trifling sum regularly, the aggregate making a handsome sum for the family of each member who passeth to the beyond. This do I see as something desirable and which I could highly recommend. But today it is not possible because it must reach beyond the life of any man or any partnership to operate. It must be as stable as the King's throne. Someday do I feel that such a plan shall come to pass and be a great blessing to many men, because even the first small payment will make available a snug fortune for the family of a member should he pass on.

'But because we live in our own day and not in the days which are to come, must we take advantage of those means and ways of accomplishing our purposes. Therefore do I recommend to all men, that they, by wise and well thought out methods, do provide against a lean purse in their mature years. For a lean purse to a man no longer able to earn or to a family without its head is a sore tragedy.

'This, then, is the sixth cure for a lean purse. Provide in advance for the needs of thy growing age and the protection of thy family.'

THE SEVENTH CURE
Increase thy ability to earn

'This day do I speak to thee, my students, of one of the most vital remedies for a lean purse. Yet, I will talk not of gold but of yourselves, of the men beneath the robes of many colours who do sit before me. I will talk to you of those things within the minds and lives of men which do work for or against their success.' So did Arkad address his class upon the seventh day.

'Not long ago came to me a young man seeking to borrow. When I questioned him the cause of his necessity, he complained that his earnings were insufficient to pay his expenses. Thereupon I explained to him, this being the case, he was a poor customer for the moneylender, as he possessed no surplus earning capacity to repay the loan.

'What you need, young man,' I told him, 'is to earn more coins. What dost thou to increase thy capacity to earn?'

'All that I can do' he replied.

'Six times within two moons have I approached my master to request my pay be increased, but without success. No man can go oftener than that.'

'We may smile at his simplicity, yet he did possess one of the vital requirements to increase his earnings. Within him was a strong desire to earn more, a proper and commendable desire.

'*Preceding accomplishment must be desire. Thy desires must be strong and definite.* General desires are but weak longings. For a man to wish to be rich is of little purpose. For a man to desire five pieces of gold is a tangible desire which he can press to fulfilment. After he has backed his desire for five pieces of gold with strength of purpose to secure it, next he can find similar ways to obtain ten pieces and then twenty pieces and later a thousand pieces and, behold, he has become wealthy. In learning to secure his one definite small desire, he hath trained himself to secure a larger one. This is the process by which wealth is accumulated: first in small sums, then in larger ones as a man learns and becomes more capable.

'Desires must be simple and definite. They defeat their own purpose should they be too many, too confusing, or beyond a man's training to accomplish.

'As a man perfecteth himself in his calling even so doth his ability to earn increase. In those days when I was a humble scribe carving upon the clay for a few coppers each day, I observed that other workers did more than I and were paid more. Therefore, did I determine that I would be exceeded by none. Nor did it take long for me to discover the reason for their greater success. More interest in my work, more concentration upon my task, more persistence in my effort, and, behold, few men could carve more tablets in a day than I. With reasonable promptness my increased skill was rewarded, nor was it necessary for me to go six times to my master to request recognition.

'The more of wisdom we know, the more we may earn. That man who seeks to learn more of his craft shall be richly rewarded. If he is an artisan, he may seek to learn the methods and the tools of those most skillful in the same line. If he laboureth at the law or at healing, he may consult and exchange knowledge with others of his calling. If he be a merchant, he may continually seek better goods that can be purchased at lower prices.

'Always do the affairs of man change and improve because keen-minded men seek greater skill that they may better serve those upon whose patronage they depend. Therefore, I urge all men to be in the front rank of progress and not to stand still, lest they be left behind.

'Many things come to make a man's life rich with gainful experiences. Such things as the following, a man must do if he respect himself:

He must pay his debts with all the promptness within his power, not purchasing that for which he is unable to pay.

'He must take care of his family that they may think and speak well of him.

'He must make a will of record that, in case the Gods

call him, proper and honourable division of his property be accomplished.

'He must have compassion upon those who are injured and smitten by misfortune and aid them within reasonable limits. He must do deeds of thoughtfulness to those dear to him.

'Thus the seventh and last remedy for a lean purse is *to cultivate thy own powers, to study and become wiser, to become more skillful, to so act as to respect thyself. Thereby shalt thou acquire confidence in thy self to achieve thy carefully considered desires.*

'These then are the seven cures for a lean purse, which, out of the experience of a long and successful life, I do urge for all men who desire wealth.

'There is more gold in Babylon, my students, than thou dreamest of. There is abundance for all.

'Go thou forth and practice these truths that thou mayest prosper and grow wealthy, as is thy right.

'Go thou forth and teach these truths that every honourable subject of his majesty may also share liberally in the ample wealth of our beloved city.'

14

Kahlil Gibran

The Prophet

Lebanese-American poet Kahlil Gibran is best-known for his collection of vivid and striking prose-poetry fables, The Prophet, *which happens to be one of the most translated books in the world. In this excerpt, the Prophet reflects on the symbiotic relationship between business and well-being of society. He underlines the importance of fair trade in transactions, cautioning against greed and imbalance.*

~

ON BUYING AND SELLING

And a merchant said, speak to us of buying and selling.

And he answered and said:

To you the earth yields her fruit, and you shall not want if you but know how to fill your hands.

It is in exchanging the gifts of the earth that you shall find abundance and be satisfied.

Yet unless the exchange be in love and kindly justice, it will but lead some to greed and others to hunger.

When in the marketplace you toilers of the sea and fields and vineyards meet the weavers and the potters and the gatherers of spices—

Invoke then the master spirit of the earth, to come into your midst and sanctify the scales and the reckoning that weighs value against value. And suffer not the barren-handed to take part in your transactions, who would sell their words for your labour.

To such men you should say,

'Come with us to the field, or go with our brothers to the sea and cast your net;

For the land and the sea shall be bountiful to you even as to us.'

And if there come the singers and the dancers and the flute players—buy of their gifts also.

For they too are gatherers of fruit and frankincense, and that which they bring, though fashioned of dreams, is raiment and food for your soul.

And before you leave the market place, see that no one has gone his way with empty hands.

For the master spirit of the earth shall not sleep peacefully upon the wind till the needs of the least of you are satisfied.

15

Henry Thomas Hamblin

Within You Is the Power

An English mystic and pioneer of the New Thought Movement, Henry Thomas Hamblin wrote extensively on nurturing the mind and spirit and manifesting positivity. Here he tells us that true success is not solely measured by wealth or fame but helping others and contributing to the common good.

~

SUCCESS

What is meant here by success is the achievement of something worthwhile, that shall make the world better and richer, and add something to the common good. Our sphere in life may be very humble, but if we overcome our own weaknesses, help others along life's pathway, and do our daily work better than we need, our life cannot be other than successful. If, at the end of our life, we can be thankful for it, realizing that we have made the best possible use of it, we have achieved real success.

Success, to the unillumined, may mean the accumulation of wealth and the winning of fame. Yet those who give up their lives to the acquirement of these things are the greatest failures in life. They gain wealth, it is true, but they find that their money can buy only those things that bring no satisfaction: that it cannot purchase for them any of the things which are really worth having. Success of this hollow kind, can be won, but at too great a price. The greatest Teacher of all once said: 'For what shall it profit man, if he shall gain the whole world and lose his own soul?' What *does* it profit a man if he 'gets on' at the cost of happiness, health, joy of living, domestic life, and the ability to appreciate Nature's beauties and simple pleasures?

Yet man must be a striver. He must be for ever seeking better things and to express himself more perfectly. One who drifts through life, making no effort to rise to better things, is not worthy of the name of citizen. Man, if he is to be worthy of the name, must be for ever striving, overcoming, rising. Failure in life is always due to weakness of character. It is only strong characters who can resist the buffetings of life and overcome its difficulties. The man who would make his life worthy of respect and who would rise to high achievement and service, will be confronted by difficulty at every turn. This is as it should be, for it weeds out the weaklings and unworthy aspirants, and awards the spoils to those who exhibit faith, courage, steadfastness, patience, perseverance, persistence, cheerfulness, and strength of character, generally. Success, especially material success, is not, in itself, of much benefit to the one who wins it. It does not satisfy for long, but it is valuable in other ways. For instance, success, based on service, is a benefit to the community. If, it were not for successful people of this type the ordinary man in the rut would have a bad time. Also, the winning of success builds up character. One who would be successful in the battle of life, must be prepared to be tested and tried in every possible way. One who survives them all is built up in character in almost every direction. Even in his success, however, he will be tempted and tried. One who is engaged in the harsh struggle of business, or who takes part in public life, may, if he does not watch himself very carefully, become hard and callous. Of all failures this is probably the worst. One who succeeds in other directions and becomes a 'hard man', is, after all, a sorry failure.

Life is a continual battle. To the ordinary person it is generally a fight with circumstances and the ordinary difficulties of life which are very important in his eyes. The more advanced soul is not troubled much by these things—he rises above them—but he is tempted and tried to a much greater degree, and in a far more subtle manner. Those who think that by following a certain 'cult' or 'ism', they will be able to have an uneventful walk through life are merely deluding themselves. As he learns to overcome the difficulties of life which baffle the ordinary individual, he will be tempted and tried in other and more subtle ways. This is because life is not for mere passing pleasure, but is for the building up of character, through experience. Therefore, one who would succeed must be strong, and wise and patient. Those who aspire to make their lives really worthwhile: who desire to serve their fellows more perfectly: who want to build up character through experience and overcome all their weaknesses, inherited or otherwise, must look within for power and wisdom.

Success and achievement will not drop ready made from heaven into your lap. All who succeed are gluttons for work, toiling whilst others play and sleep. All teaching to the contrary is erroneous. To think that success is going to come to you when it is unmerited, simply because you make use of 'affirmations' or employ mental 'treatments', is folly of the first water. On the other hand, to use the inner forces in an occult way, so as to compel material things or 'success', so-called, in any shape or form, to come to you, is black magic. One who stoops to such practices becomes a black magician, earning for himself a terrible retribution. There is only one way to succeed in the affairs of life, and that is by raising oneself to greater usefulness and service. By doing things better than they have been done before, by bearing greater responsibility, you serve humanity better, and therefore merit success. 'It is more blessed to give than to receive,' said the Master, and this is true even in the practical and material affairs of life. First, you must give better and more valuable service: in other words, deserve and merit before you expect to see it materialize. You must sow before you can reap: you must become too big for your present position before you are capable of occupying a larger one. You must grow and expand in every possible way, and as you grow so will your success increase. Outward success is only a reflection, so to speak, of what you really are, and a result of greater and more valuable service to humanity. It requires great effort and determination to get out of the rut, but so long as your ambition is not ignoble or selfish, there will be found within you power sufficient for all your needs.

To win success, either in the hurly-burly of life, or the more difficult path of spiritual progress, demands imagination, vision, courage, faith, determination, persistence, perseverance, hope, cheerfulness, and other qualities. These are all to be found within. All these qualities lie more or less dormant within, and can be called into expression if we believe that Infinite Power is ours.

Again, however, must the warning be repeated that this Power must not be used for selfish self-aggrandizement, still less may it be used, or, rather, mis-used, either to influence or dominate others. If this Power is mis-used the results are terrible and disastrous. Therefore, use the Power only for the achievement of good and noble aims and in service which shall enrich the life of your fellows, adding to the common good. Having arrived at this stage you must go forward. There can be no holding back. Ever onward, the Divine Urge is sending you, to greater achievement and accomplishment. Just as surely as the planets must revolve round the sun and fulfil their destiny, so also must you go forward. See to it, then, that your aims and ambitions are based upon eternal wisdom, for upon this does your whole future depend.

16

Napoleon Hill

Think and Grow Rich

Taken from Napoleon Hill's magnum opus Think and Grow Rich, *this passage highlights the distinction between general and specialized knowledge, emphasizing that it is the zest for learning and the strategic acquisition of ideas that leads one to heights of success.*

~

SPECIALIZED KNOWLEDGE, PERSONAL EXPERIENCE, OR OBSERVATIONS

There are two kinds of knowledge. One is general, the other is specialized. General knowledge, no matter how great in quantity or variety it may be, is of but little use in the accumulation of money. The faculties of the great universities possess, in the aggregate, practically every form of general knowledge known to civilization. Most of the professors have but little or no money. They specialize on teaching knowledge, but they do not specialize on the organization, or the use of knowledge.

Knowledge will not attract money, unless it is organized, and intelligently directed, through practical PLANS OF ACTION, to the DEFINITE END of accumulation of money. Lack of understanding of this fact has been the source of confusion to millions of people who falsely believe that 'knowledge is power.' It is nothing of the sort! Knowledge is only potential power. It becomes power only when, and if, it is organized into definite plans of action, and directed to a definite end.

This 'missing link' in all systems of education known to civilization today, may be found in the failure of educational institutions to teach their students.

How to Organize and Use Knowledge
After They Acquire It

Many people make the mistake of assuming that, because Henry Ford had but little 'schooling,' he is not a man of 'education.' Those who make this mistake do not know Henry Ford, nor do they understand the real meaning of the word 'educate.'

That word is derived from the Latin word 'educo,' meaning to educe, to draw out, to DEVELOP FROM WITHIN. An educated man is not, necessarily, one who has an abundance of general or specialized knowledge. An educated man is one who has so developed the faculties of his mind that he may acquire anything he wants, or its equivalent, without violating the rights of others. Henry Ford comes well within the meaning of this definition.

During the world war, a Chicago newspaper published certain editorials in which, among other statements, Henry Ford was called 'an ignorant pacifist.' Mr Ford objected to the statements, and brought suit against the paper for libeling him.

When the suit was tried in the Courts, the attorneys for the paper pleaded justification, and placed Mr Ford, himself, on the witness stand, for the purpose of proving to the jury that he was ignorant. The attorneys asked Mr Ford a great variety of questions, all of them intended to prove, by his own evidence, that, while he might possess considerable specialized knowledge pertaining to the manufacture of automobiles, he was, in the main, ignorant.

Mr Ford was plied with such questions as the following: 'Who was Benedict Arnold?' and 'How many soldiers did the British send over to America to put down the Rebellion of 1776?' In answer to the last question, Mr Ford replied, 'I do not know the exact number of soldiers the British sent over, but I have heard that it was a considerably larger number than ever went back.'

Finally, Mr Ford became tired of this line of questioning, and in reply to a particularly offensive question, he leaned over, pointed his finger at the lawyer who had asked the question, and said, 'If I should really WANT to answer the foolish question you have just asked, or any of the other questions you have been asking me, let me remind you that I have a row of electric push-buttons on my desk, and by pushing the right button, I can summon to my aid men who can answer ANY question I desire to ask concerning the business to which I am devoting most of my efforts. Now, will you kindly tell me, WHY I should clutter up my mind with general knowledge, for the purpose of being able to answer questions, when I have men around me who can supply any knowledge I require?' There certainly was good logic to that reply. That answer floored the lawyer. Every person in the courtroom realized it was the answer, not of an ignorant man, but of a man of EDUCATION. Any man is educated who knows where to get knowledge when he needs it, and how to organize that knowledge into definite plans of action.

Through the assistance of his 'Master Mind' group, Henry Ford had at his command all the specialized knowledge he needed to enable him to become one of the wealthiest men in America. It was not essential that he have this knowledge in his own mind. Surely no person who has sufficient inclination and intelligence to read a book of this nature can possibly miss the significance of this illustration.

Before you can be sure of your ability to transmute DESIRE into its monetary equivalent, you will require SPECIALIZED KNOWLEDGE of the service, merchandise, or profession which you intend to offer in return for fortune. Perhaps you may need much more specialized knowledge than you have the ability or the inclination to acquire, and if this should be true, you may bridge your weakness through the aid of your 'Master Mind' group.

Andrew Carnegie stated that he, personally, knew nothing about the technical end of the steel business; moreover, he did not particularly care to know anything about it. The specialized knowledge which he required for the manufacture and marketing of steel, he found available through the individual units of his MASTER MIND GROUP.

The accumulation of great fortunes calls for POWER, and power is acquired through highly organized and intelligently directed specialized knowledge, but that knowledge does not, necessarily, have to be in the possession of the man who accumulates the fortune.

The preceding paragraph should give hope and encouragement to the man with ambition to accumulate a fortune, who has not possessed himself of the necessary 'education' to supply such specialized knowledge as he may require. Men sometimes go through life suffering from 'inferiority complexes,' because they are not men of 'education.' The man who can organize and direct a 'Master Mind' group of men who possess knowledge useful in the accumulation of money, is just as much a man of education as any man in the group. REMEMBER THIS, if you suffer from a feeling of inferiority, because your schooling has been limited.

Thomas A. Edison had only three months of 'schooling' during his entire life. He did not lack education, neither did he die poor. Henry Ford had less than a sixth grade 'schooling' but he has managed to do pretty well by himself, financially.

SPECIALIZED KNOWLEDGE is among the most plentiful, and the cheapest forms of service which may be had! If you doubt this, consult the payroll of any university.

It Pays to Know How to Purchase Knowledge

First of all, decide the sort of specialized knowledge you require, and the purpose for which it is needed. To a large extent your major purpose in life, the goal toward which you are working, will help determine what knowledge you need. With this question settled, your next move requires that you have accurate information concerning dependable sources of knowledge. The more important of these are:

(a) One's own experience and education
(b) Experience and education available through cooperation of others
(c) Colleges and universities
(d) Public libraries (through books and periodicals in which may be found all the knowledge organized by civilization)
(e) Special training courses

As knowledge is acquired it must be organized and put into use, for a definite purpose, through practical plans. Knowledge has no value except that which can be gained from its application toward some worthy end. This is one reason why college degrees are not valued more highly. They represent nothing but miscellaneous knowledge.

If you contemplate taking additional schooling, first determine the purpose for which you want the knowledge you are seeking, then learn where this particular sort of knowledge can be obtained, from reliable sources. Successful men, in all callings, never stop acquiring specialized knowledge related to their major purpose, business, or profession. Those who are not successful usually make the mistake of believing that the knowledge acquiring period ends when one finishes school. The truth is that schooling does but little more than to put one in the way of learning how to acquire practical knowledge.

The person who stops studying merely because he has finished school is forever hopelessly doomed to mediocrity, no matter what may be his calling. The way of success is the way of continuous pursuit of knowledge. Let us consider a specific instance. During the depression a salesman in a grocery store found himself without a position. Having had some bookkeeping experience, he took a special course in accounting, familiarized himself with all the latest bookkeeping and office equipment, and went into business for himself. Starting with the grocer for whom he had formerly worked, he made contracts with more than 100 small merchants to keep their books, at a very nominal monthly fee. His idea was so practical that he soon found it necessary to set up a portable office in a light delivery truck, which he equipped with modern bookkeeping machinery. He now has a fleet of these bookkeeping offices 'on wheels' and employs a large staff of assistants, thus providing small merchants with accounting service equal to the best that money can buy, at very nominal cost.

Specialized knowledge, plus imagination, were the ingredients that went into this unique and successful business. Capability means IMAGINATION, the one quality needed to combine specialized knowledge with IDEAS, in the form of ORGANIZED PLANS designed to yield riches.

17

William George Jordan

The Majesty of Calmness: Individual Problems and Possibilities

*Although written in an American context, the excerpt from
the author's bestselling book provides an invaluable lesson in
the pitfalls of achieving wealth in a hurry and how the rush to
accumulate riches causes more harm than good. It highlights
the detrimental effects of hurry on all aspects of life,
advocating for a slower, more deliberate approach to work,
relationships, and personal development.*

~

HURRY, THE SCOURGE OF AMERICA

The first sermon in the world was preached at the Creation. It was a Divine protest against Hurry. It was a Divine object lesson of perfect law, perfect plan, perfect order, perfect method. Six days of work carefully planned, scheduled and completed were followed by—rest. Whether we accept the story as literal or as figurative, as the account of successive days or of ages comprising millions of years, matters little if we but learn the lesson.

Nature is very un-American. Nature never hurries. Every phase of her working shows plan, calmness, reliability, and the absence of hurry. Hurry always implies lack of definite method, confusion, impatience of slow growth. The Tower of Babel, the world's first skyscraper, was a failure because of hurry. The workers mistook their arrogant ambition for inspiration. They had too many builders—and no architect. They thought to make up the lack of a head by a superfluity of hands. This is a characteristic of Hurry. It seeks ever to make energy a substitute for a clearly defined plan—the result is ever as hopeless as trying to transform a hobby-horse into a real steed by brisk riding.

Hurry is a counterfeit of haste. Haste has an ideal, a distinct aim to be realized by the quickest, direct methods. Haste has a single compass upon which it relies for direction and in harmony with which its course is determined. Hurry says: 'I must move faster. I will get three compasses; I will have them different; I will be guided by all of them. One of them will probably be right.' Hurry never realizes that slow, careful foundation work is the quickest in the end.

Hurry has ruined more Americans than has any other word in the vocabulary of life. It is the scourge of America; and is both a cause and a result of our high-pressure civilization. Hurry adroitly assumes so many masquerades of disguise that its identity is not always recognized.

Hurry always pays the highest price for everything, and, usually the goods are not delivered. In the race for wealth men often sacrifice time, energy, health, home, happiness and honour—everything that money cannot buy, the very things that money can never bring back. Hurry is a phantom of paradoxes. Business men, in their desire to provide for the future happiness of their family, often sacrifice the present happiness of wife and children on the altar of Hurry. They forget that their place in the home should be something greater than being merely 'the man that pays the bills;' they expect consideration and thoughtfulness that they are not giving.

We hear too much of a wife's duties to a husband and too little of the other side of the question. 'The wife,' they tell us, 'should meet her husband with a smile and a kiss, should tactfully watch his moods and be ever sweetness and sunshine.' Why this continual swinging of the censer of devotion to the man of business? Why should a woman have to look up with timid glance at the face of her husband, to 'size up his mood'? Has not her day, too, been one of care, and responsibility, and watchfulness? Has not mother-love been working over perplexing problems and worries of home and of the training of the children that wifely love may make her seek to solve in secret? Is man, then, the weaker sex that he must be pampered and treated as tenderly as a boil trying to keep from contact with the world?

In their hurry to attain some ambition, to gratify the dream of a life, men often throw honour, truth, and generosity to the winds. Politicians dare to stand by and see a city poisoned with foul water until they 'see where they come in' on a water-works appropriation. If it be necessary to poison an army—that, too, is but an incident in the hurry for wealth.

This is the Age of the Hothouse. The element of natural growth is pushed to one side and the hothouse and the force-pump are substituted. Nature looks on tolerantly as she says: 'So far you may go, but no farther, my foolish children.'

The educational system of to-day is a monumental institution dedicated to Hurry. The children are forced to go through a series of studies that sweep the circle of all human wisdom. They are given everything that the ambitious ignorance of the age can force into their minds; they are taught everything but the essentials—how to use their senses and how to think. Their minds become congested by a great mass of undigested facts, and still the cruel, barbarous forcing goes on. You watch it until it seems you cannot stand it a moment longer, and you instinctively put out your hand and say: 'Stop! This modern slaughter of the Innocents must *not* go on!' Education smiles suavely, waves her hand complacently toward her thousands of knowledge-prisons over the country, and says: 'Who are you that dares speak a word against our sacred, school system?' Education is in a hurry. Because she fails in fifteen years to do what half the time should accomplish by better methods, she should not be too boastful. Incompetence is not always a reason for pride. And they hurry the children into a hundred textbooks, then into ill-health, then into the colleges, then into a diploma, then into life—with a dazed mind, untrained and unfitted for the real duties of living.

Hurry is the deathblow to calmness, to dignity, to poise. The old-time courtesy went out when the new-time hurry came in. Hurry is the father of dyspepsia. In the rush of our national life, the bolting of food has become a national vice. The words 'Quick Lunches' might properly be placed on thousands of headstones in our cemeteries. Man forgets that he is the only animal that dines; the others merely feed. Why does he abrogate his right to dine and go to the end of the line with the mere feeders? His self-respecting stomach rebels, and expresses its indignation by indigestion. Then man has to go through life with a little bottle of pepsin tablets in his vest-pocket. He is but another victim to this craze for speed. Hurry means the breakdown of the nerves. It is the royal road to nervous prostration.

Everything that is great in life is the product of slow growth; the newer, and greater, and higher, and nobler the work, the slower is its growth, the surer is its lasting success. Mushrooms attain their full power in a night; oaks require decades. A fad lives its life in a few weeks; a philosophy lives through generations and centuries. If you are sure you are right, do not let the voice of the world, or of friends, or of family swerve you for a moment from your purpose. Accept slow growth if it must be slow, and know the results *must* come, as you would accept the long, lonely hours of the night—with absolute assurance that the heavy-leaded moments *must* bring the morning.

Let us as individuals banish the word 'hurry' from our lives. Let us care for nothing so much that we would pay honour and self-respect as the price of hurrying it. Let us cultivate calmness, restfulness, poise, sweetness—doing our best, bearing all things as bravely as we can; living our life undisturbed by the prosperity of the wicked or the malice of the envious. Let us not be impatient, chafing at delay, fretting over failure, wearying over results, and weakening under opposition. Let us ever turn our face toward the future with confidence and trust, with the calmness of a life in harmony with itself, true to its ideals, and slowly and constantly progressing toward their realization.

Let us see that cowardly word Hurry in all its most degenerating phases, let us see that it ever kills truth, loyalty, thoroughness; and let us determine that, day by day, we will seek more and more to substitute for it the calmness and repose of a true life, nobly lived.

18

Orison Swett Marden

The Victorious Attitude

In this excerpt from his highly acclaimed book, the author advocates for cultivating a mindset of abundance and shaping our thoughts to weed out negativity, visualize triumph, and manifest the best lives for ourselves. This way, individuals become magnets for success and build a prosperous path free of financial burdens.

~

MAKING YOURSELF A PROSPERITY MAGNET

Though culture is the most important business of life. The habit of claiming as our own, as a vivid, present reality that which we desire with all our heart, is a magnetic power which attracts the things we long for. The more persistently we hold the prosperity thought, the more we strengthen and intensify it, the more we increase its power to attract prosperity.

Thinking abundance, visualizing prosperity, will open up the mind, and set the thought currents toward increased supply.

We are so made that about all we get in life is the reflex of what first flows out from us. Whatever thought you send out will draw to you in the material world a corresponding reality.

Every human being is a magnet, the attractive power of which may be developed in any desired direction. Each one can so direct this power that he can draw to himself whatever he wills.

Before your life can be really effective you must make yourself a magnet for the things that will make it so. You must learn how to attract, how to draw to yourself all that will help you to succeed in your work, that will enable you to attain your ambitions.

If poverty is holding you down, you can conquer it by making yourself a prosperity magnet. We are living in the midst of a stream of inexhaustible supply. It is one's own fault if he does not take from this stream whatever he needs.

What we get in life we get by the law of attraction. Like attracts like. Whatever you may have managed to get together in this world you have attracted by your mentality. You may say that you have earned these things, that you have bought them with your salary, the fruit of your endeavour. True, but your thought preceded your endeavour. Your mental plan went before your achievement.

The mere changing of your mental attitude will very soon begin to change conditions. Your decision to face toward prosperity hereafter, to cultivate it, to make yourself a prosperity magnet will tend to draw to you the things that will satisfy your ambition.

If you want to become a prosperity magnet you must not only think prosperity but you must also turn your back resolutely on poverty. Begin today. Don't wait for tomorrow. or next day. If you don't look prosperous, assume a prosperous appearance. Dress as far as possible like a prosperous man or woman, walk like one, act like one, think in terms of prosperity.

The same thing is true in curing yourself of poverty. You can not do this as long as you hold poverty-stricken conditions in your mind. If you want to be prosperous you must hold the prosperous thought, the prosperous picture in your mind. You must refuse to see or recognize poverty. You must not acknowledge it in your manner. You must erase all marks of it, not only from your mental attitude, but just as far as possible from your appearance. Even if you are not able to wear fine clothes at first, or to live in a fine house, you can radiate the hope and expectancy of the glorious inheritance which is your birthright, and everything about you will reflect this light.

Prosperity begins in the mind. You must lay its foundations in your thoughts, surround yourself with a prosperity atmosphere. In other words, you will build into your environment, into your life, whatever dwells in your mind.

We hear of some people that 'they are always lucky'; 'everything seems to come their way'. Things come their way because there are invisible thought forces radiating from their minds toward the goal they have set for themselves. Things fall in line and come our way just in proportion to the force and velocity of the thought forces we project.

The truth is we were all intended to live the life abundant. The Creator never meant His children to grovel in poverty, to spend their lives in drudgery and uncertainty. They have a right to their inheritance of all that is good and beautiful, all that is needful for their welfare. We were not intended to live the pinched, starved, stunted lives of paupers. It is our own fault if we do. The door to opulence is open to every human being born into this world, and no one but himself can close that door. No human being can shut out the lowliest child that is born from his divine inheritance. The only real poverty is in the mind, and no one can control one's mind but himself.

Turn your back on poverty. Make up your mind that you will never again have anything to do with it, that you will not encourage it by dwelling on and visualizing poverty suggestions. Face toward prosperity. Think of, and plan for prosperous conditions; struggle toward prosperity with all your might and you will draw it to you.

Tidy up your little home and make it as neat and cheerful as possible. Do the same with your dress and general appearance. Keep yourself better groomed; look up, brace up, brush up, struggle up. Surround yourself with an atmosphere of hopefulness and show everybody by the new light in your eyes, the light of hope and expectancy of better things, that there is a change in you. Your neighbours will notice it. They will see a change in your home, in your wife, in your children. The change in the mental attitude of yourself and family, through facing toward the light instead of darkness, toward hope instead of despair, will make a tremendous change in your whole outlook on life.

In this way you are making yourself a prosperity magnet; you are radiating thought waves of hope, of ambition, of determination. Your new mental attitude is expressed in an erect, manly carriage, in squared, thrown back shoulders, in a neat, clean appearance, even though the clothing be old and threadbare, in a winning, forceful, magnetic countenance. You are thus establishing the conditions of success. The positive prosperity thought flows out like a wireless current and connects itself with similar thought currents. Hold the prosperity conviction, work steadily toward your object; see opportunity and success in your vista, determine to be somebody, hold firmly to the resolve, and your mentality will direct the invisible magnet of your personality to lift you higher and higher, to attract toward you others who will help you in the direction in which you are moving.

Abundance will never flow through pinched, doubting, poverty thoughts, any more than clear, crystal water can flow freely through foul, grease-clogged pipes. A right viewpoint must be your mental plumber to keep the connection open and free. Things of a kind attract one another. The poverty thought attracts more poverty, the fear thought more fear, the worry thought more worry, the anxiety thought more anxiety. On the other hand, the faith thought, trust thought, and the confidence thought attract things like themselves.

Poverty is a disease that can only be cured by prosperity remedies. The prosperity thought is the natural antidote for the poverty germ. It kills it. The poverty thought cannot exist in the mind at the same moment with the prosperity thought. One will drive out the other. It rests with you which one you will harbor and encourage.

Cling to the consciousness of your oneness with the All-Supply. Keep the supply pipes between you and the Infinite Source of all good always open. Don't pinch them. Don't cut off the supply by the limiting poverty thought, the doubt thought, the fear thought, the worry thought. Keep your supply pipes open by great faith in your Father-Mother-God, who is more solicitous for your welfare than any human parent could be. Hold fast to the anchor of your union with the Infinite Life; keep in the current running Godward and your life will not dry up or become barren, will not be blighted and blasted by the poverty drought.

You must think in a positive determined way that you are going to succeed in whatever you desire to do or to be before you can expect success. That is the first condition by which you make yourself a magnet for the thing you are after. It doesn't matter whether it is work or money, a better position or health, or whatever else it is, your thoughts about it must be positive, clean cut, decisive, persistent. No weak, wobbly 'Perhaps I may get it,' or 'Maybe it will come some time,' or 'I wonder if I shall get this,' or 'if I can do that' sort of thought will ever help you to get anything in this world or the next.

Hold the victorious attitude toward life and you will overcome all unfavourable conditions.

19

Earl Prevette

How to Turn Your Ability into Cash

In this chapter, Earl Prevette discusses the importance of turning financial success into lasting gains and opportunities. Highlighting the need for caution and increased vigilance as one progresses professionally, the author provides useful pointer such as taking small steps to save money, watching out for profitable opportunities, and practicing economy to prepare for future responsibilities.

~

How to Turn Your Ability into Cash will also show you, once you have got a foothold, how to turn your cash into ability.

I here refer to the accumulative talent that knows how to consolidate its gains and convert them into new accessions of profit.

Money makes money and your first small success will open up new avenues and opportunities for making more. That is how great corporations and great fortunes grow.

How to Increase Your Initial Gains

Making a profit in your initial venture is neither so difficult nor so exciting as progressing from profit to profit in subsequent efforts. It is not so difficult because you have something to work with. It is not so exciting because now you are gunning for bigger game.

Do not misunderstand that previous paragraph. First success is sweet. There is something about it that does not come again. I simply want to make the point that there is a greater thrill in bagging a tiger than in shooting a jack rabbit.

But a tiger hunt is dangerous. The bigger the game, the bigger the risk. An important banker told me years ago that it was astounding how many men who succeed in getting a financial start, proceed to dissipate their original stake through a lack of caution.

Caution should be increased, not relaxed, as our responsibilities and resources overlap and grow. We should guard against the complacency induced by success and cultivate and exercise the utmost vigilance in our transactions. For, money is vulnerable and the more we have, the more we are subject to the envy and the wiles of those who covet it. But conserve and protect it and the opportunities for increasing it are manifold.

Large Returns from Small Investments

Nobody knows how many businesses, great and small, have been founded or enabled to survive by some man who had money available when another man needed it. One man's necessity is another man's opportunity. I know of a number of cases where even limited funds, which were available as ready cash, have enabled men to reap rewards out of all proportion to the sums involved. The man who needs financial assistance must meet the terms of the man who supplies it. That is one of the immutable laws of money, whether thousands or millions are at stake.

Some years ago a manufacturer in New York, whose business, then recently started, showed a great promise of success, but whose resources were inadequate to develop it, was in desperate need of $25,000. A man I know, who had worked and struggled for seven years to accumulate just that amount, made a deal that gave him one-third ownership. This share during the past six years has returned him $25,000 annually. Another acquaintance of mine put $15,000 into a small chain-store enterprise and in five years got his money back ten times over. And these are but two minor instances of the major role played by ready cash in the rescue of the man who is short of it.

'Watch the Basket'

Save your money and watch for opportunities to get it to work at a profit. Then continue to watch it for your protection. Be cautious in choosing your investments and vigilant in supervising them. Carnegie said : 'Put all your eggs in one basket and watch the basket.' Maybe that was good advice in his particular case because he was referring to steel, in which he was at the time America's most competent and powerful authority. He controlled the industry and could speak with knowledge and assurance. Personally, I recommend a little variety in the baskets, but in any event the second half of the warning still holds: 'Watch the basket'.

And meanwhile, do not be discouraged because at present you have little or nothing to put into the basket. The important thing is to make a beginning, and the best beginning is to cultivate and practice economy in small matters to prepare yourself for future financial responsibilities. The trouble with most of us is that, in our quest of great gains, we are prone to ignore, or neglect, the little things that so often lead on to fortune.

Many years ago, a small boy applied for a vacancy in a Paris bank. His services were not acceptable. On his way out of the bank he suddenly stopped and stooped to pick up something from the floor. The man who had just dismissed him, probably wondering if the boy had found something of value, called him back and questioned him. The boy took from the lapel of his coat about the simplest, and certainly the cheapest, commodity on earth: an ordinary pin! He had learned economy the hard way. An impoverished home had taught him that even so small an item as a common pin was important in the struggle for survival. He was immediately hired and that was the beginning of a great financial career. He became the famous French banker Lafitte.

.20.

Samuel Smiles

Character

In this passage, the author focusses on the transformative power of work, describing it as a vital life force that greatly helps in cultivating obedience, self-control, and perseverance. He encourages the idea that work contributes to personal happiness, societal well-being, and even the stability of nations, stressing on the role of industry in both individual fulfilment and common progress.

~

WORK

Work is one of the best educators of practical character. It evokes and disciplines obedience, self-control, attention, application, and perseverance; giving a man deftness and skill in his special calling, and aptitude and dexterity in dealing with the affairs of ordinary life.

Work is the law of our being—the living principle that carries men and nations onward. The greater number of men have to work with their hands, as a matter of necessity, in order to live; but all must work in one way or another, if they would enjoy life as it ought to be enjoyed.

Labour may be a burden and a chastisement, but it is also an honour and a glory. Without it, nothing can be accomplished. All that is great in man comes through work; and civilization is its product. Were labour abolished, the race of Adam were at once stricken by moral death.

It is idleness that is the curse of man—not labour. Idleness eats the heart out of men as of nations, and consumes them as rust does iron. When Alexander conquered the Persians, and had an opportunity of observing their manners, he remarked that they did not seem conscious that there could be anything more servile than a life of pleasure, or more princely than a life of toil.

Indolence is equally degrading to individuals as to nations. Sloth never made its mark in the world, and never will. Sloth never climbed a hill, nor overcame a difficulty that it could avoid. Indolence always failed in life, and always will. It is in the nature of things that it should not succeed in anything. It is a burden, an incumbrance, and a nuisance—always useless, complaining, melancholy, and miserable.

Burton, in his quaint and curious, book—the only one, Johnson says, that ever took him out of bed two hours sooner than he wished to rise—describes the causes of melancholy as hinging mainly on idleness. 'Idleness,' he says, 'is the bane of body and mind, the nurse of naughtiness, the chief mother of all mischief, one of the seven deadly sins, the devil's cushion, his pillow and chief repose.... An idle dog will be mangy; and how shall an idle person escape? Idleness of the mind is much worse than that of the body: wit, without employment, is a disease— the rust of the soul, a plague, a hell itself. As in a standing pool, worms and filthy creepers increase, so do evil and corrupt thoughts in an idle person; the soul is contaminated.... Thus much I dare boldly say: he or she that is idle, be they of what condition they will, never so rich, so well allied, fortunate, happy—let them have all things in abundance and felicity that heart can wish and desire, all contentment—so long as he, or she, or they, are idle, they shall never be pleased, never well in body or mind, but weary still, sickly still, vexed still, loathing still, weeping, sighing, grieving, suspecting, offended with the world, with every object, wishing themselves gone or dead, or else carried away with some foolish phantasie or other.'

Burton says a great deal more to the same effect; the burden and lesson of his book being embodied in the pregnant sentence with which it winds up:—'Only take this for a corollary and conclusion, as thou tenderest thine own welfare in this, and all other melancholy, thy good health of body and mind, observe this short precept, Give not way to solitariness and idleness. BE NOT SOLITARY—BE NOT IDLE.'

The indolent, however, are not wholly indolent. Though the body may shirk labour, the brain is not idle. If it do not grow corn, it will grow thistles, which will be found springing up all along the idle man's course in life. The ghosts of indolence rise up in the dark, ever staring the recreant in the face, and tormenting him:

> *'The gods are just, and of our pleasant vices,*
> *Make instrument to scourge us.'*

True happiness is never found in torpor of the faculties, but in their action and useful employment. It is indolence that exhausts, not action, in which there is life, health, and pleasure. The spirits may be exhausted and wearied by employment, but they are utterly wasted by idleness. Hence a wise physician was accustomed to regard occupation as one of his most valuable remedial measures. 'Nothing is so injurious,' said Dr Marshall Hall, 'as unoccupied time.' An archbishop of Mayence used to say that 'the human heart is like a millstone: if you put wheat under it, it grinds the wheat into flour; if you put no wheat, it grinds on, but then 'tis itself it wears away.'

Indolence is usually full of excuses; and the sluggard, though unwilling to work, is often an active sophist. 'There is a lion in the path' or 'The hill is hard to climb' or 'There is no use trying—I have tried, and failed, and cannot do it'. To the sophistries of such an excuser, Sir Samuel Romilly once wrote to a young man:— 'My attack upon your indolence, loss of time was most serious, and I really think that it can be to nothing but your habitual want of exertion that can be ascribed your using such curious arguments as you do in your defence. Your theory is this: Every man does all the good that he can. If a particular individual does no good, it is a proof that he is incapable of doing it. That you don't write proves that you can't; and your want of inclination demonstrates your want of talents. What an admirable system!—and what beneficial effects would it be attended with, if it were but universally received!'

It has been truly said, that to desire to possess, without being burdened with the trouble of acquiring, is as much a sign of weakness, as to recognize that everything worth having is only to be got by paying its price, is the prime secret of practical strength. Even leisure cannot be enjoyed unless it is won by effort. If it have not been earned by work, the price has not been paid for it.

There must be work before and work behind, with leisure to fall back upon; but the leisure, without the work, can no more be enjoyed than a surfeit. Life must needs be disgusting alike to the idle rich man as to the idle poor man, who has no work to do, or, having work, will not do it. The words found tattooed on the right arm of a sentimental beggar of forty, undergoing his eighth imprisonment in the gaol of Bourges in France, might be adopted as the motto of all idlers: 'LE PASSE M'A TROMPE; LE PRESENT ME TOURMENTE; L'AVENIR M'EPOUVANTE' (the past has deceived me; the present torments me; the future terrifies me).

Constant, useful occupation is thus wholesome, not only for the body, but for the mind. While the slothful man drags himself indolently through life, and the better part of his nature sleeps a deep sleep, if not morally and spiritually dead, the energetic man is a source of activity and enjoyment to all who come within reach of his influence. Even any ordinary drudgery is better than idleness.

We have spoken of work as a discipline: it is also an educator of character. Even work that produces no results, because it is work, is better than torpor—inasmuch as it educates faculty, and is thus preparatory to successful work. The habit of working teaches method. It compels economy of time, and the disposition of it with judicious forethought. And when the art of packing life with useful occupations is once acquired by practice, every minute will be turned to account; and leisure, when it comes, will be enjoyed with all the greater zest.

Coleridge has truly observed, that 'if the idle are described as killing time, the methodical man may be justly said to call it into life and moral being, while he makes it the distinct object not only of the consciousness, but of the conscience. He organizes the hours and gives them a soul; and by that, the very essence of which is to fleet and to have been, he communicates an imperishable and spiritual nature. Of the good and faithful servant, whose energies thus directed are thus methodized, it is less truly affirmed that he lives in time than that time lives in him. His days and months and years, as the stops and punctual marks in the record of duties performed, will survive the wreck of worlds, and remain extant when time itself shall be no more.'

To conclude: a fair measure of work is good for mind as well as body. Man is an intelligence sustained and preserved by bodily organs, and their active exercise is necessary to the enjoyment of health. It is not work, but overwork, that is hurtful; and it is not hard work that is injurious so much as monotonous work, fagging work, hopeless work. All hopeful work is healthful; and to be usefully and hopefully employed is one of the great secrets of happiness. Brain-work, in moderation, is no more wearing than any other kind of work. Duly regulated, it is as promotive of health as bodily exercise; and, where due attention is paid to the physical system, it seems difficult to put more upon a man than he can bear. Merely to eat and drink and sleep one's way idly through life is vastly more injurious. The wear-and-tear of rust is even faster than the tear-and-wear of work.

But overwork is always bad economy. It is, in fact, great waste, especially if conjoined with worry. Indeed, worry kills far more than work does. It frets, it excites, it consumes the body—as sand and grit, which occasion excessive friction, wear out the wheels of a machine. Overwork and worry have both to be guarded against. For over-brain-work is strain-work; and it is exhausting and destructive according as it is in excess of nature. And the brain-worker may exhaust and overbalance his mind by excess, just as the athlete may overstrain his muscles and break his back by attempting feats beyond the strength of his physical system.

SECTION III

DEALING WITH HARDSHIP

.21.

James Allen

As a Man Thinketh

Excerpted from James Allen's most famous work, As a Man
Thinketh, *this passage extols the virtue of calmness, deeming it as
one of man's greatest possessions that arises from practicing self-
control and understanding of thought. The author believes that a
serene individual, adept at governing his emotions and adapting to
others, fosters a balanced, well-poised character.*

~

SERENITY

Calmness of mind is one of the beautiful jewels of wisdom.
It is the result of long and patient effort in self-control. Its
presence is an indication of ripened experience, and of a more
than ordinary knowledge of the laws and operations of thought.

A man becomes calm in the measure that he understands
himself as a thought evolved being, for such knowledge
necessitates the understanding of others as the result of
thought, and as he develops a right understanding, and sees
more and more clearly the internal relations of things by the
action of cause and effect he ceases to fuss and fume and worry
and grieve, and remains poised, steadfast, serene.

The calm man, having learned how to govern himself,
knows how to adapt himself to others; and they, in turn,
reverence his spiritual strength, and feel that they can learn of
him and rely upon him. The more tranquil a man becomes, the

greater is his success, his influence, his power for good. Even the ordinary trader will find his business prosperity increase as he develops a greater self-control and equanimity, for people will always prefer to deal with a man whose demeanour is strongly equable.

The strong, calm man is always loved and revered. He is like a shade-giving tree in a thirsty land, or a sheltering rock in a storm. 'Who does not love a tranquil heart, a sweet-tempered, balanced life? It does not matter whether it rains or shines, or what changes come to those possessing these blessings, for they are always sweet, serene, and calm. That exquisite poise of character, which we call serenity is the last lesson of culture, the fruitage of the soul. It is precious as wisdom, more to be desired than gold—yea, than even fine gold. How insignificant mere money seeking looks in comparison with a serene life—a life that dwells in the ocean of Truth, beneath the waves, beyond the reach of tempests, in the eternal calm!'

'How many people we know who sour their lives, who ruin all that is sweet and beautiful by explosive tempers, who destroy their poise of character, and make bad blood! It is a question whether the great majority of people do not ruin their lives and mar their happiness by lack of self-control. How few people we meet in life who are well balanced, who have that exquisite poise which is characteristic of the finished character!'

Yes, humanity surges with uncontrolled passion, is tumultuous with ungoverned grief, is blown about by anxiety and doubt only the wise man, only he whose thoughts are controlled and purified, makes the winds and the storms of the soul obey him.

Tempest-tossed souls, wherever ye may be, under whatsoever conditions ye may live, know this: in the ocean of life the isles of Blessedness are smiling, and the sunny shore of your ideal awaits your coming. Keep your hand firmly upon the helm of thought. In the back of your soul, reclines the commanding Master; He does but sleep: wake Him. Self-control is strength; Right Thought is mastery; Calmness is power. Say unto your heart, 'Peace, be still!'

22

Olivia Ward Bush-Banks

A Picture

Born in Sag Harbor, New York, in 1869, Olivia Ward Bush-Banks was the daughter of African–American and Montauk parents. Her poems frequently reflected on her heritage and biracial identity. In this poem, she conveys a longing for a brighter, more optimistic portrayal of existence. The dark sea, sombre rocks, and troubled clouds convey misfortunes, while ships navigating through suggest life's changing scenes. The poet expresses a desire to repaint the picture with a serene sea, clear sky, and swift, joyous ships.

~

I drew a picture long ago—
A picture of a sullen sea;
A picture that I value now
Because it clears Life's mystery.

My sea was dark and full of gloom;
I painted rocks of sombre hue.
My sky alone bespoke of light,
And that I painted palest blue.

But e'en across my sky of blue
Stretched troubled clouds of sodden gray,
Through which the sun shone weak and dim,
With only here and there a ray.

Around my rocks the yellow foam
Seemed surging, moaning in despair
As if the waves, their fury spent,
Left naught but desolation there.

Three crafts with fluttering sails I drew,
And one sailed near the rocks of gray,
The other on its westward course,
Went speeding out of danger's way.

The other still outdistanced them
Where sky and water seemed to met.
I painted that with sails full set,
And then my picture was complete.

My life was like the sullen sea,
Misfortunes, woes, my rocks of gray,
The crafts portrayed Life's changing scenes,
The clouded sky Life's troubled Day.

I longed to paint that picture o'er
Without the rocks of sombre hue;
Without the troubled clouds of gray,
I'll paint the sky of brightest blue.

My sea shall lay in calm repose,
No hint of surging, moaning sigh.
My crafts, unhindered by the rocks,
Shall speed in joyous swiftness by.

But this shall be when brightest hours
Of hope and cheer are given me.
I'll paint this picture when Life's sun
Shines clear upon Prosperity.

23

Dale Carnegie

How to Stop Worrying and Start Living

The author recounts a dramatic story told by Robert Moore, who learned a profound lesson during the intense moments when his submarine was under attack. The terror he experienced taught him how trivial worries, such as those about work or domestic issues, seemed insignificant in the face of life-threatening danger. The author underscores the importance of shifting perspective and not allowing small concerns to dominate one's thoughts and emotions.

~

DON'T LET THE BEETLES GET YOU DOWN

Here is a dramatic story that I'll probably remember as long as I live. It was told to me by Robert Moore, of 14 Highland Avenue, Maplewood, New Jersey.

'I learned the biggest lesson of my life in March, 1945,' he said, 'I learned it under 276 feet of water off the coast of Indo-China. I was one of eighty-eight men aboard the submarine Baya S.S. 318. We had discovered by radar that a small Japanese convoy was coming our way. As daybreak approached, we submerged to attack. I saw through the periscope a Jap destroyer escort, a tanker, and a minelayer.

We fired three torpedoes at the destroyer escort, but missed. Something went haywire in the mechanics of each torpedo. The destroyer, not knowing that she had been attacked, continued on. We were getting ready to attack the last ship, the minelayer, when suddenly she turned and came directly at us. (A Jap plane had spotted us under sixty feet of water and had radioed our position to the Jap minelayer.) We went down to 150 feet, to avoid detection, and rigged for a depth charge. We put extra bolts on the hatches; and, in order to make our sub absolutely silent, we turned off the fans, the cooling system, and all electrical gear.

'Three minutes later, all hell broke loose. Six depth charges exploded all around us and pushed us down to the ocean floor—a depth of 276 feet. We were terrified. To be attacked in less than a thousand feet of water is dangerous—less than five hundred feet is almost always fatal. And we were being attacked in a trifle more than half of five hundred feet of water—just about knee-deep, as far as safety was concerned. For fifteen hours, that Jap minelayer kept dropping depth charges. If a depth charge explodes within seventeen feet of a sub, the concussion will blow a hole in it. Scores of these depth charges exploded within fifty feet of us. We were ordered 'to secure'—to lie quietly in our bunks and remain calm. I was so terrified I could hardly breathe. 'This is death,' I kept saying to myself over and over. 'This is death! This is death!' With the fans and cooling system turned off, the air inside the sub was over a hundred degrees; but I was so chilled with fear that I put on a sweater and a fur-lined jacket; and still I trembled with cold. My teeth chattered. I broke out in a cold, clammy sweat. The attack continued for fifteen hours. Then ceased suddenly. Apparently the Jap minelayer had exhausted its supply of depth charges, and steamed away. Those fifteen hours of attack seemed like fifteen million years. All my life passed before me in review.

I remembered all the bad things I had done, all the little absurd things I had worried about. I had been a bank clerk before I joined the Navy. I had worried about the long hours, the poor pay, the poor prospects of advancement. I had worried because I couldn't own my own home, couldn't buy a new car, couldn't buy my wife nice clothes. How I had hated my old boss, who was always nagging and scolding! I remembered how I would come home at night sore and grouchy and quarrel with my wife over trifles. I had worried about a scar on my forehead—a nasty cut from an auto accident.

'How big all these worries seemed years ago! But how absurd they seemed when depth charges were threatening to blow me to kingdom come. I promised myself then and there that if I ever saw the sun and the stars again, I would never, never worry again. Never! Never! I Never! I learned more about the art of living in those fifteen terrible hours in that submarine than I had learned by studying books for four years in Syracuse University.'

We often face the major disasters of life bravely—and then let the trifles, the 'pains in the neck', get us down. For example, Samuel Pepys tells in his Diary about seeing Sir Harry Vane's head chopped off in London. As Sir Harry mounted the platform, he was not pleading for his life, but was pleading with the executioner not to hit the painful boil on his neck!

That was another thing that Admiral Byrd discovered down in the terrible cold and darkness of the polar nights—that his men fussed more about the 'pains in the neck' than about the big things. They bore, without complaining, the dangers, the hardships, and the cold that was often eighty degrees below zero. 'But,' says Admiral Byrd, 'I know of bunkmates who quit speaking because each suspected the other of inching his gear into the other's allotted space; and I knew of one who could not eat unless he could find a place in the mess hall out of sight of the Fletcherist who solemnly chewed his food twenty-eight times before swallowing.

'In a polar camp,' says Admiral Byrd, 'little things like that have the power to drive even disciplined men to the edge of insanity.'

And you might have added, Admiral Byrd, that 'little things' in marriage drive people to the edge of insanity and cause 'half the heartaches in the world.'

At least, that is what the authorities say. For example, Judge Joseph Sabath of Chicago, after acting as arbiter in more than forty thousand unhappy marriages, declared: 'Trivialities are at the bottom of most marital unhappiness'; and Frank S. Hogan, District Attorney of New York County, says: 'Fully half the cases in our criminal courts originate in little things. Bar-room bravado, domestic wrangling, an insulting remark, a disparaging word, a rude action—those are the little things that lead to assault and murder. Very few of us are cruelly and greatly wronged. It is the small blows to our self-esteem, the indignities, the little jolts to our vanity, which cause half the heartaches in the world.'

When Eleanor Roosevelt was first married, she 'worried for days' because her new cook had served a poor meal. 'But if that happened now,' Mrs Roosevelt says, 'I would shrug my shoulders and forget it.' Good. That is acting like an adult emotionally. Even Catherine the Great, an absolute autocrat, used to laugh the thing off when the cook spoiled a meal.

Mrs Carnegie and I had dinner at a friend's house in Chicago. While carving the meat, he did something wrong. I didn't notice it; and I wouldn't have cared even if I had noticed it. But his wife saw it and jumped down his throat right in front of us. 'John,' she cried, 'watch what you are doing! Can't you ever learn to serve properly!'

Then she said to us: 'He is always making mistakes. He

just doesn't try.' Maybe he didn't try to carve; but I certainly give him credit for trying to live with her for twenty years. Frankly, I would rather have eaten a couple of hot dogs with mustard—in an atmosphere of peace—than to have dined on Peking duck and shark fins while listening to her scolding.

Shortly after that experience, Mrs Carnegie and I had some friends at our home for dinner. Just before they arrived, Mrs Carnegie found that three of the napkins didn't match the tablecloth.

'I rushed to the cook,' she told me later, 'and found that the other three napkins had gone to the laundry. The guests were at the door. There was no time to change. I felt like bursting into tears! All I could think was: 'Why did this stupid mistake have to spoil my whole evening?' Then I thought—well why let it? I went in to dinner, determined to have a good time. And I did. I would much rather our friends think I was a sloppy housekeeper,' she told me, 'than a nervous, bad-tempered one. And anyhow, as far as I could make out, no one noticed the napkins!'

A well-known legal maxim says: De minimis non curat lex: 'the law does not concern itself with trifles.' And neither should the worrier—if he wants peace of mind.

Much of the time, all we need to overcome the annoyance of trifles is to affect a shifting of emphasis set up a new, and pleasurable, point of view in the mind. My friend Homer Croy, who wrote They Had to See Paris and a dozen other books, gives a wonderful example of how this can be done. He used to be driven half crazy, while working on a book, by the rattling of the radiators in his New York apartment. The steam would bang and sizzle—and he would sizzle with irritation as he sat at his desk.

'Then,' says Homer Croy, 'I went with some friends on a

camping expedition. While listening to the limbs crackling in the roaring fire, I thought how much they sounded like the crackling of the radiators. Why should I like one and hate the other? When I went home I said to myself: 'The crackling of the limbs in the fire was a pleasant sound; the sound of the radiators is about the same—I'll go to sleep and not worry about the noise.' And I did. For a few days I was conscious of the radiators; but soon I forgot all about them.

'And so it is with many petty worries. We dislike them and get into a stew, all because we exaggerate their importance....'

Disraeli said: 'Life is too short to be little.' 'Those words,' said Andre Maurois in *This Week* magazine, 'have helped me through many a painful experience: often we allow ourselves to be upset by small things we should despise and forget.... Here we are on this earth, with only a few more decades to live, and we lose many irreplaceable hours brooding over grievances that, in a year's time, will be forgotten by us and by everybody. No, let us devote our life to worth-while actions and feelings, to great thoughts, real affections and enduring undertakings. For life is too short to be little.'

Even so illustrious a figure as Rudyard Kipling forgot at times that 'Life is too short to be little'. The result? He and his brother-in-law fought the most famous court battle in the history of Vermont—a battle so celebrated that a book has been written about it: Rudyard Kipling's Vermont Feud.

The story goes like this: Kipling married a Vermont girl, Caroline Balestier, built a lovely home in Brattleboro, Vermont; settled down and expected to spend the rest of his life there. His brother-in-law, Beatty Balestier, became Kipling's best friend. The two of them worked and played together.

Then Kipling bought some land from Balestier, with the understanding that Balestier would be allowed to cut hay off it each season. One day, Balestier found Kipling laying out a flower garden on this hayfield. His blood boiled. He hit the ceiling. Kipling fired right back. The air over the Green Mountains of Vermont turned blue!

A few days later, when Kipling was out riding his bicycle, his brother-in-law drove a wagon and a team of horses across the road suddenly and forced Kipling to take a spill. And Kipling the man who wrote: 'If you can keep your head when all about you are losing theirs and blaming it on you'—he lost his own head, and swore out a warrant for Balestier's arrest. A sensational trial followed. Reporters from the big cities poured into the town. The news flashed around the world. Nothing was settled. This quarrel caused Kipling and his wife to abandon their American home for the rest of their lives. All that worry and bitterness over a mere trifle! A load of hay.

Pericles said, twenty-four centuries ago: 'Come, gentlemen, we sit too long on trifles.' We do, indeed! Here is one of the most interesting stories that Dr Harry Emerson Fosdick ever told—a story about the battles won and lost by a giant of the forest:

On the slope of Longs Peak in Colorado lies the ruin of three gigantic trees. Naturalists tell us that it stood for some four hundred years. It was a seedling when Columbus landed at San Salvador, and half grown when the Pilgrims settled at Plymouth. During the course of its long life it was struck by lightning fourteen times, and the innumerable avalanches and storms of four centuries thundered past it. It survived them all. In the end, however, an army of beetles attacked the tree and levelled it to the ground. The insects ate their way through the bark and gradually destroyed the inner strength of the tree by their tiny but incessant attacks. A forest giant which age had not withered, nor lightning blasted, nor storms subdued, fell at last before beetles so small that a man could crush them between his forefinger and his thumb.

Aren't we all like that battling giant of the forest? Don't we manage somehow to survive the rare storms and avalanches and lightning blasts, only to let our hearts be eaten out by little beetles of worry, little beetles that could be crushed between a finger and a thumb?

To break the worry habit before it breaks you, here is: let's not allow ourselves to be upset by small things we should despise and forget. Remember: 'Life is too short to be little.'

Emily Dickinson

Hope Is the Thing with Feathers

Written by one of the greatest poets of the nineteenth century,
Hope Is the Thing with Feathers *by Emily Dickinson is a*
poem that conveys how hope is always present, resilient,
and enduring, much like a bird that never stops singing.
It can be found in the toughest conditions and remains
steadfast even in the stormiest weather, thereby uplifting
the human spirit in the darkest of times.

~

'Hope' is the thing with feathers —
That perches in the soul—
And sings the tune without the words —
And never stops—at all—

And sweetest—in the Gale—is heard —
And sore must be the storm—
That could abash the little Bird
That kept so many warm—

I've heard it in the chillest land —
And on the strangest Sea—
Yet—never—in Extremity,
It asked a crumb—of me.

Henry Thomas Hamblin

Within You Is the Power

In this lesson, the author asserts that life's true purpose is the attainment of wisdom, and this will be achieved by facing challenges with conviction and faith and rejecting the notion of an easy life as an illusion. The key to happiness is recognizing the power within ourselves and moving away from shortcuts that only promise a temporary respite from our troubles.

~

OVERCOMING LIFE'S DIFFICULTIES

The true object of life is that man may attain wisdom through experience. This cannot be accomplished by giving in to the difficulties of life, but only by overcoming them. The promises of God are not made to those who fail in life's battle, but to those who overcome. Neither are there any promises that man shall have an easy time and be happy ever afterwards. Yet, it is after this that the majority of people are for ever seeking—an easy life, a good time, freedom from suffering and care. But, in spite of all their seeking, they can never find that which they desire. There is always a fly in the ointment of their pleasure, something that robs them of true happiness; or, possibly, combinations of circumstances conspire to upset all their plans.

Life is a paradox; the true object of life is not the attainment of happiness, yet if we attain the true object of life we find happiness. Those who are ignorant of life's true purpose and who seek happiness high and low, year after year, fail to find it. Like a will-o'-the-wisp, it for ever eludes them. On the other hand, those who recognize the true object of life, and follow it, attain happiness without seeking for it.

In times past, people have made God a convenience. They have thought they could drift through life, learning none of its discipline and then, when in trouble, or things were not to their liking, they could pray to God and have the unpleasant circumstances taken away. The same idea is prevalent to-day. People have left the old orthodoxy and look to various 'cults' and 'isms' to get them out of their difficulties. They do not believe now that they can curry special favour with God by prayer, but they firmly believe that they can get what they want from the Invisible by demanding it. They think that by this means they can have their own way after all. By this they mean having a good time, with no unpleasant experiences, trials, difficulties, adversities. They are, however, merely chasing rainbows. The easy life they seek constantly eludes them, simply because there is no such thing. The only life that is easy is the life of the strong soul who has overcome. His life is not easy in reality, but appears relatively so because of his strength.

It is impossible to have an easy life, and, if it were possible, then life would be not worth living, for the sole object of life is the building of character and the attainment of wisdom through experience. Life to all of us must always be full of difficulty, and it is to help those, who, hitherto, have found life rather too much for them that this book is being written. What the majority are seeking for is an easy life (which they will never find, but precisely the reverse) and for them I have no message. But to those wise and awakened souls who are seeking for Truth, no matter from whence it may come, and who desire to overcome life and its difficulties, instead of weakly giving in to them, this book, it is hoped, will bring a message.

At this stage we cannot go into the subject of why we should meet with disasters and adversity in this life, nor why some people should have, apparently, a smoother life than others. We must therefore be satisfied to know that we have to meet trouble and overcome difficulty, and that it is only by so doing that we can attain wisdom and build up character. The question, then, is not whether we shall meet the trouble and adversity or not, but rather, how we shall meet them. Shall we be victorious or shall we be submerged? Shall we overcome life's difficulties or shall we give in to them?

The majority of people are drifters on the sea of life. They are wafted here and blown there: they are also carried hither and thither by every current. It is only the few who realize that they have the Power of the Infinite within them by which they can rise superior to all their difficulties, overcome their own weaknesses, and, through victorious experience, attain wisdom.

At this point some practical reader may say that attaining wisdom is all very well, but what he wants is practical help. He is perhaps out of work, has sickness in his house and is in debt. Or, he may be well-to-do, and yet in the deepest distress and misery. To all such I would say that they possess the Power by which they can overcome all their difficulties, and, through overcoming, attain wisdom. A man's success depends, more than anything, upon his faith—his faith in the good purpose of life: his faith in the Power of the Infinite within him and his ability to overcome every obstacle in his path.

The extent of the Power that man can bring into his life is the measure of his faith in that Power. If his faith in it is small, then his life will be feeble and lacking in achievement.

If his faith in the Power within him is large, then great will be the power manifesting in his life. The Power of the Infinite is illimitable and inexhaustible: all that is required is an unquenchable belief and trust in it. The weakest and most timid can make use of this Power. There is the same Power in the timid and weak as in the brave and strong. The weakness of the former is due to a lack of faith and belief in the Infinite Power within them.

Difficulties and troubles there will be in every life, and sometimes disaster and heartbreak, when the very earth slides from under the feet, yet, by calling upon the Power within, it is possible to rise from the ruins of cherished hopes stronger and 'greater' through experience. Happiness and true success depend upon how the troubles and difficulties of life are met. Adversity comes to all, but if it is met in the right manner even failure can be made the stepping-stone to success. Trouble comes to all, but, while it makes some people stronger and better in every way, it submerges others so that they never rise again. The trouble is the same, it is how it is met that makes the difference. Those who meet difficulty and adversity in the feeble strength of their finite minds and false personality are speedily overwhelmed and broken by the storms of life. But those who rely upon, and have faith in the Power within them, can never be overwhelmed, neither can they ever be defeated. The Power, being infinite, is always sufficient, no matter how great the need may be.

One who realizes his own real spiritual identity, knows that he can never die, that he can never be defeated, that he can never really fail. He may lose his body through the change that is called death; but he, the true man, can never die. Neither can he fail, though he be defeated a thousand times—he must rise again.

Orison Swett Marden

Pushing to the Front

In this lesson, the author emphasizes the significance of hard work and determination in achieving any feat, whether great or small. Through anecdotes of celebrated personalities, he highlights the idea that achievements arise from not waiting for opportunities but learning from setbacks and persisting in the pursuits for true and earned success.

~

SUCCESS UNDER DIFFICULTIES

'I have here three teams that I want to get over to Staten Island,' said a boy of twelve one day in 1806 to the innkeeper at South Amboy, N. J. 'If you will put us across, I'll leave with you one of my horses in pawn, and if I don't send you back six dollars within forty-eight hours you may keep the horse.'

The innkeeper asked the reason for this novel proposition, and learned that the lad's father had contracted to get the cargo of a vessel stranded near Sandy Hook, and take it to New York in lighters. The boy had been sent with three wagons, six horses, and three men, to carry the cargo across a sand-spit to the lighters. The work accomplished, he had started with only six dollars to travel a long distance home over the Jersey sands, and reached South Amboy penniless. 'I'll do it,' said the innkeeper, as he looked into the bright honest eyes of the boy. The horse was soon redeemed.

'My son,' said this same boy's mother, on the first of May, 1810, when he asked her to lend him one hundred dollars to buy a boat, having imbibed a strong liking for the sea; 'on the twenty-seventh of this month you will be sixteen years old. If, by that time, you will plow, harrow, and plant with corn the eight-acre lot, I will advance you the money.' The field was rough and stony, but the work was done in time, and well done. From this small beginning Cornelius Vanderbilt laid the foundation of a colossal fortune.

In 1818 Vanderbilt owned two or three of the finest coasting schooners in New York harbour, and had a capital of nine thousand dollars. Seeing that steam-vessels would soon win supremacy over those carrying sails only, he gave up his fine business to become the captain of a steamboat at one thousand dollars a year. For twelve years he ran between New York City and New Brunswick, N. J. In 1829 he began business as a steamboat owner, in the face of opposition so bitter that he lost his last dollar. But the tide turned, and he prospered so rapidly that he at length owned over a hundred steamboats. He early identified himself with the growing railroad interests of the country, and became the richest man of his day in America.

Barnum began the race of business life barefoot, for at the age of fifteen he was obliged to buy on credit the shoes he wore at his father's funeral. He was a remarkable example of success under difficulties. There was no keeping him down; no opposition daunted him.

'Eloquence must have been born with you,' said a friend to J. P. Curran. 'Indeed, my dear sir, it was not,' replied the orator; 'it was born some three and twenty years and some months after me.' Speaking of his first attempt at a debating club, he said: 'I stood up, trembling through every fibre; but remembering that in this I was but imitating Tully, I took courage and had actually proceeded almost as far as 'Mr Chairman,' when, to my astonishment and terror, I perceived that every eye was turned on me. There were only six or seven present, and the room could not have contained as many more; yet was it, to my panic-stricken imagination, as if I were the central object in nature, and assembled millions were gazing upon me in breathless expectation. I became dismayed and dumb. My friends cried, 'Hear him!' but there was nothing to hear. He was nicknamed 'Orator Mum,' and well did he deserve the title until he ventured to stare in astonishment at a speaker who was 'culminating chronology by the most preposterous anachronisms'. 'I doubt not,' said the annoyed speaker, 'that "Orator Mum" possesses wonderful talents for eloquence, but I would recommend him to show it in future by some more popular method than his silence.' Stung by the taunt, Curran rose and gave the man a 'piece of his mind,' speaking fluently in his anger. Encouraged by this success, he took great pains to become a good speaker. He corrected his habit of stuttering by reading favourite passages aloud every day slowly and distinctly, and spoke at every opportunity.

Bunyan wrote his *Pilgrim's Progress* on the untwisted papers which were used to cork the bottles of milk brought for his meals. Gifford wrote his first copy of a mathematical work, when a cobbler's apprentice, on small scraps of leather; and Rittenhouse, the astronomer, first calculated eclipses on his plow handle.

'All the performances of human art, at which we look with praise and wonder,' says Johnson, 'are instances of the resistless force of perseverance: it is by this that the quarry becomes a pyramid, and that distant countries are united with canals. If a man was to compare the effect of a single stroke of the pickax, or of one impression of the spade, with the general design and last result, he would be overwhelmed by the sense of their disproportion; yet those petty operations, incessantly continued, in time surmount the greatest difficulties, and mountains are levelled, and oceans bounded, by the slender force of human beings.'

Great men never wait for opportunities; they make them. Nor do they wait for facilities or favouring circumstances; they seize upon whatever is at hand, work out their problem, and master the situation. A young man determined and willing will find a way or make one. A Franklin does not require elaborate apparatus; he can bring electricity from the clouds with a common kite.

Great men have found no royal road to their triumph. It is always the old route, by way of industry and perseverance.

Nearly every great discovery or invention that has blessed mankind has had to fight its way to recognition, even against the opposition of the most progressive men.

William H. Prescott was a remarkable example of what a boy with 'no chance' can do. While at college, he lost one eye by a hard piece of bread thrown during a 'biscuit battle,' and the other eye became almost useless. But the boy would not lead a useless life. He set his heart upon being a historian, and turned all his energies in that direction. By the aid of others' eyes, he spent ten years studying before he even decided upon a particular theme for his first book. Then he spent ten years more, poring over old archives and manuscripts, before he published his *Ferdinand and Isabella*. What a lesson in his life for young men! What a rebuke to those who have thrown away their opportunities and wasted their lives!

There is no open door to the temple of success. Everyone who enters makes his own door, which closes behind him to all others, not even permitting his own children to pass.

Not in the brilliant salon, not in the tapestried library, not in ease and competence, is genius born and nurtured; but often in adversity and destitution, amidst the harassing cares of a straitened household, in bare and fireless garrets. Amid scenes unpropitious, repulsive, wretched, have men laboured, studied, and trained themselves, until they have at last emanated from the gloom of that obscurity the shining lights of their times; have become the companions of kings, the guides and teachers of their kind, and exercised an influence upon the thought of the world amounting to a species of intellectual legislation.

Columbus was dismissed as a fool from court after court, but he pushed his suit against an incredulous and ridiculing world. Rebuffed by kings, scorned by queens, he did not swerve a hair's breadth from the overmastering purpose which dominated his soul. The words 'New World' were graven upon his heart; and reputation, ease, pleasure, position, life itself if need be, must be sacrificed. Threats, ridicule, ostracism, storms, leaky vessels, mutiny of sailors, could not shake his mighty purpose.

You cannot keep a determined man from success. Place stumbling-blocks in his way and he takes them for stepping-stones, and on them will climb to greatness. Take away his money, and he makes spurs of his poverty to urge him on. Cripple him, and he writes the *Waverley* novels.

All that is great and noble and true in the history of the world is the result of infinite painstaking, perpetual plodding, of common everyday industry.

.27.

Joseph Murphy

The Power of Your Subconscious Mind

Joseph Murphy was an Irish author who spent a significant amount of time in India studying Hindu philosophy. His most famous book, The Power of Your Subconscious Mind, *has been a perennial bestseller in India and elsewhere. Through an anecdote about a son looking for his father's will, he tells us how to make a difficult decision without losing our cool or getting flustered thinking about the multiple outcomes of the situation.*

~

HOW TO RECEIVE GUIDANCE
FROM YOUR SUBCONSCIOUS

When you have what you term 'a difficult decision' to make, or when you fail to see the solution to your problem, begin at once to think constructively about it. If you are fearful and worried, you are not really thinking. True thinking is free from fear. Here is a simple technique you can use to receive guidance on any subject: quiet the mind and still the body. Tell the body to relax; it has to obey you. It has no volition, initiative, or self-conscious intelligence. Your body is an emotional disk, which records your beliefs and impressions. Mobilize your attention; focus your thought on the solution to your problem. Try to solve it with your conscious mind. Think how happy you would be about the perfect solution. Sense the feeling you would have if the perfect answer were yours now. Let your mind play with this mood in a relaxed way; then drop off to sleep. When you awaken, and you do not have the answer, get busy about something else. Probably, when you are preoccupied with something else, the answer will come into your mind like toast pops out of a toaster.

In receiving guidance from the subconscious mind, the simple way is the best. This is an illustration: I once lost a valuable ring, which was an heirloom. I looked everywhere for it and could not locate it. At night I talked to the subconscious in the same manner that I would talk to anyone. I said to it prior to dropping off to sleep, 'You know all things; you know where that ring is, and you now reveal to me where it is.' In the morning I awoke suddenly with the words ringing in my ear, 'Ask Robert!' I thought it very strange that I should ask Robert, a young boy about nine years of age; however, I followed the inner voice of intuition. Robert said, 'Oh, yes, I picked it up in the yard while I was playing with the boys. I placed it on the desk in my room. I did not think it worth anything, so I did not say anything about it.' The subconscious mind will always answer you if you trust it.

The Secret of Guidance

The secret of guidance or right action is to mentally devote yourself to the right answer, until you find its response in you. The response is a feeling, an inner awareness, and an overpowering hunch whereby you know that you know. You have used the power to the point where it begins to use you. You cannot possibly fail or make one false step while operating under the subjective wisdom within you. You will find that all your ways are pleasantness and all your paths are peace.

Highlights to Recall

1. Remember that the subconscious mind has determined the success and wonderful achievements of all great scientific workers.
2. By giving your conscious attention and devotion to the solution of a perplexing problem, your subconscious mind gathers all the necessary information and presents it full-blown to the conscious mind.
3. If you are wondering about the answer to a problem, try to solve it objectively. Get all the information you can from research and also from others. If no answer comes, turn it over to your subconscious mind prior to sleep, and the answer always comes. It never fails.
4. You do not always get the answer overnight. Keep on turning your request over to your subconscious until the daybreaks and the shadows flee away.

28

Earl Prevette

How to Turn Your Ability into Cash

Recounting an encounter with a destitute old man in Philadelphia, the author explores the destructive impact of negative thoughts on one's life, leading to despair, discouragement, and even physical ailments. Comparing positive thoughts to the power of light dispelling darkness, he calls for the eradication of patterns that hold us back from unlocking one's full potential and achieve success we incessantly desire.

~

IT MIGHT HAVE BEEN YOU

One day not long ago, while I was standing on the corner of a busy street in Philadelphia, talking to a friend, along came an old man. He was a decrepit old man with swollen, tearful, eyes, and his unshaven face was drawn and withered. His lips were blue with unclean sores. His toes were pushing through his worn-out shoes. His clothes were torn to rags. He had seen better days. I thought, 'How dreadfully poverty has gnawed at you.' I was stunned for the moment. With a look of sadness, and with a dirty, bloated hand thrust forward, he pleaded for a few pennies. He got a few more pennies; I got a little more sense.

As I pondered over the circumstances that had caused the deplorable condition of this man, and had left him a wreck in its ruins, I began to think: 'It might have been you!'

What happened to this old man? What started him toward his deplorable condition? What caused such poverty? Why had fortune turned into misfortune? His plight may have been due to overindulgence, to grief, to envy, to jealousy, to hatred, to prejudice, to dread, to self-pity, to temptation, or to discouragement. Whatever it was, it had changed his outlook, his attitude, his process of thinking, and his entire pattern of living. Desperation, despair, discouragement, disappointment, sorrow, and sadness were indelibly stamped in the lines of his face. He was a picture of his thoughts, a victim of circumstances, and a slave to poverty.

Your Greatest Enemy

In analysing the plight of this old man, I came to the conclusion that his condition was a definite result of that desperate little enemy—negative thinking.

Negative thinking is a sneaky little enemy that silently steals its way into a man's consciousness and, like a thief at night steals not his purse but, through robbing him of power, makes him poor indeed. Negative thinking is a sinister influence that works night and day to prey on a man's soul. It is man's worst enemy, and life's meanest foe. It is worse than war, and largely the cause of war. It is the curse of the human race. It is as blind to reason as an owl is to light. It turns friends into enemies and enemies into foes. It robs a man of reason. It stirs up hate, greed, selfishness, cynicism, pessimism, anger, suspicion, rivalry, jealousy, revenge, lust, and envy. It tears down confidence, undermines health, impairs character, and causes poverty.

An old legend relates that the devil was thrown into bankruptcy. Out of all his tools, the creditors permitted him to keep one. The tool he selected was the wedge of negative thinking. Asked why he liked this tool better than all the rest, the devil explained, 'It is because this is the one tool which I can use when all others fail. Let me get that little wedge into a man's consciousness, and it opens everything else. That wedge has opened more doors for me than all other weapons combined.'

Someone asked one of the world's greatest explorers what exploration he enjoyed most. His answer was, 'My personal preference is for sitting in an old-fashioned rocking chair and exploring the undiscovered regions inside my own mind.'

In exploring the undiscovered regions inside the mind, man discovers he has interest. His interest creates a desire. There are two kinds of desire. One is physical. One is mental. Subsistence and propagation satisfy the physical desire. Thoughts and ideas satisfy the mental desire.

How to Conquer Negative Thinking

There are two kinds of thoughts: positive thoughts, which are creative, and negative thoughts, which are destructive. I often compare positive thoughts to light, and negative thoughts to darkness. Darkness is nothing. It is the absence of light. Turn on the light, and there is no darkness.

Negative thoughts of dread, worry, anger, prejudice, jealousy, envy, grudge, stubbornness, impudence, selfishness, cynicism, gloom, hate, despair, and discouragement disappear instantly when they meet the positive thoughts of love, faith, consideration, respect, kindness, courage, understanding, persistence, fervour, loyalty, joy, power, plenty, endurance, and strength.

Think positive thoughts, and the ability can accomplish any desire. Positive thoughts are based on understanding and doubt. Negative thoughts are based on ignorance and doubt.

There is no problem or condition that fails to disappear in the light of positive thoughts. Face one half of your problems or troubles with positive thoughts, and they will disappear, and then face the other half, and they will disappear. Positive and creative thinking will burn holes in problems, as a lighted cigarette will burn holes in tissue paper.

You are a conductor for your thoughts. Ability is the powerhouse. Positive thoughts are the current. Negative thoughts are the resistance. Get rid of all negative thoughts. Get rid of resistance. Get rid of all inhibitions, all grudges, and all dreads. Your ability demonstrates its full power and strength when unhampered, and unencumbered by resistance. Your income, your health, your well-being, your happiness, and your peace of mind are only retarded by permitting the phantoms of negative thinking to set up a resistance to your ability.

Conditions are thought-made; change your thoughts and you change your conditions. Therefore, if your conditions seem unbearable, dark, and gloomy, change your thoughts about them and see how quickly your thoughts change you.

How to Succeed Through Positive Thinking

Therefore, the remedy for negative thinking is positive thoughts. The application of positive thoughts floods the consciousness with faith, confidence, dominion, and determination and gives you the power to perform with decision, precision, skill, and speed. Think positive, be positive, and act positive, and negative thinking goes out the window. One mighty breath from Truth will scatter negative thinking and all its hosts of human mockeries and miseries like a whirlwind and establish the reign of positive thoughts that assure success in any endeavour.

How to Create Ability

Positive thoughts will knock out your worst enemy—negative thinking. The preparation is now laid for your best friend—ability. Ability is positive thoughts on the job to deliver to you the things you desire.

There is a tide in the affairs of men which when taken at the flood leads on to fortune. That tide is the accumulation of positive thoughts that must eventually burst forth into a flood of good fortune.

Emerson said, 'We lie in the lap of immense intelligence which makes us receivers of its truth, and organs of its activity. All around and about us this vital force and creative power is instantly available for us to draw from, and to apply to our activities to supply all our human needs. It is God's gift to man. It is not owned by any one man, or any group of men. It is the property of all men. However, to be of practical value, each individual must seek it, recognize it, realize it, and demonstrate it for himself in his own affairs. It is positive and active and can develop all the faculties and talents of the individual into ability capable of achievement.

'Cogito ergo sum. I think, therefore I am.' The power to think gives man the ability to analyse his own thought. Thought is not an indefinite abstraction, but a vital, living force, the most vital, subtle, and irresistible force in the world. Thought has form, quality, and substance. Thought can originate, develop, and create things.

In developing the ability to think and create things to satisfy man's desire, it is wise to get the right attitude. Man is greater than the flesh and bones that carry him around. His body belongs to him, but he does not belong to his body. The power to think does not confine him to his own skin. He can project thought. He can visualize and create things to satisfy his mental desires. To do this scientifically and effectively it is essential to organize his thoughts into a plan.

How to Turn Your Desires into Action

What is a plan? A plan is a method of action, procedure, or arrangement. It is a program to be done. It is a design to give effect to an idea, a thought, a project, or the development of something.

A plan may ask: What do you desire? Do you desire to sell something? Do you desire a job? Do you desire an increase in salary? Do you desire clients? Do you desire customers? Do you desire to invent something? These questions pertain to your present or future occupation. The only way to make your desire known is through a plan. It conveys to people in plain language a definite concept of what you are offering for their consideration.

My book, *How to Sell by Telephone*, tells how I sold $10,000,000 worth of life insurance to strangers over the telephone. To achieve this unparalleled record, it was necessary for me to create a plan to satisfy my desire. The plan set forth in plain, understandable language the value and advantages of life insurance, and what they meant to the prospect. After creating the plan it was necessary to develop a process to put the plan into action. This required faith to believe wholeheartedly in the plan, repetition to perfect it, imagination to visualize it, and persistence to see it through. Finally, it required the act to idealize the plan, to feel its possession and claim it as reality. I put all the power at my command in the plan and the desire was satisfied.

Self-discipline, self-knowledge, self-improvement, self-expression, and self-unfoldment are individual undertakings. The word 'individual' comes from two Latin words—'in', which means 'not' and 'divisus' which means 'divisible'. An individual is not divisible. He is a complete entity, a self-contained unit, made up of four parts. One part is matter—the physical body to house him. One part is essence to give him form and to identify him according to his species. One part is mind to guide and direct him. One part is spirit to inspire and to enthuse him. Strict attention and careful consideration must be given each part. The physical body must have the proper food. The essence must be treated with care. The mind must be fed with positive thoughts. The spirit must be inspired with unfaltering faith. When these four parts are well fed and well-treated, harmony prevails; and the individual functions healthfully, generates happiness and produces wealth.

Ideas and Suggestions You Can Use

First; realize that everything you can think of exists now; otherwise you could not think about it. There is no lack of anything and there should be no envy or jealousy between men. There is enough of everything for everyone that lives.

Second; realize that all things belong to God's creation and that you can only have temporary use of them. There is no limit on your desires, and you can have the use of anything the ability can create.

Third; realize that all things are distributed to those who have desires, but ability must be applied to formulate plans to claim these desires.

Here are a few suggestions that will help you stake your claim.

Things to Do

1. Meditate and ask God if there is any reason why you should not have the thing you desire. Dismiss your desire for a few days and if it is right for you to have it, the desire will become more intense. This removes doubt and uncertainty, and inspires determination and action.

2. Make a strong mental picture of what you desire, and affirm it several times each day.

3. Be specific about what you desire. If you desire money, visualize the amount and feel it in your pocket. If you desire customers, visualize the number and see them doing business with you. If you desire things, visualize the kind of thing you want and see yourself with it. If you desire a position, visualize the kind and it will soon make its appearance in your experience.

4. Relax, meditate, and be positive when you visualize your desire.

5. Be aware that ideas are infinite and the ways to manifest them are as uncountable as the stars of the heaven. Make your selection.

6. Engender a feeling of kindness into your desire. It sends out vibrations of love that are the source of attraction.

7. Thank God for the abundance that is yours now. Repeat daily.

8. Remember—an idea based on good backed by a sincere desire and held to by faith never fails to materialize.

29

Samuel Smiles

Character

*In this opening essay from his book, Samuel Smiles brings out the
paramount importance of character, the potent force that exemplifies
the best of humanity. He finds the source of all greatness to be
the consistent and sincere fulfilment of responsibility and that
contributes to the building of a strong and principled character
and a lifetime of triumphs.*

~

INFLUENCE OF CHARACTER

Character is one of the greatest motive powers in the world.
In its noblest embodiments, it exemplifies human nature in its
highest forms, for it exhibits man at his best.

Men of genuine excellence, in every station of life—men of
industry, of integrity, of high principle, of sterling honesty, of
purpose—command the spontaneous homage of mankind. It
is natural to believe in such men, to have confidence in them,
and to imitate them. All that is good in the world is upheld
by them, and without their presence in it the world would
not be worth living in.

Although genius always commands admiration, character
most secures respect. The former is more the product of brain-
power, the latter of heart-power; and in the long run it is the
heart that rules in life. Men of genius stand to society in the
relation of its intellect, as men of character of its conscience;

and while the former are admired, the latter are followed.

Great men are always exceptional men; and greatness itself is but comparative. Indeed, the range of most men in life is so limited, that very few have the opportunity of being great. But each man can act his part honestly and honourably, and to the best of his ability. He can use his gifts, and not abuse them. He can strive to make the best of life. He can be true, just, honest, and faithful, even in small things. In a word, he can do his duty in that sphere in which Providence has placed him.

Commonplace though it may appear, this doing of one's duty embodies the highest ideal of life and character. There may be nothing heroic about it; but the common lot of men is not heroic. And though the abiding sense of duty upholds man in his highest attitudes, it also equally sustains him in the transaction of the ordinary affairs of everyday existence. Man's life is 'centred in the sphere of common duties'. The most influential of all the virtues are those which are the most in request for daily use. They wear the best, and last the longest. Superfine virtues, which are above the standard of common men, may only be sources of temptation and danger. Burke has truly said that 'the human system which rests for its basis on the heroic virtues is sure to have a superstructure of weakness or of profligacy.'

Intellectual culture has no necessary relation to purity or excellence of character. In the New Testament, appeals are constantly made to the heart of man and to 'the spirit we are of', whilst allusions to the intellect are of very rare occurrence. 'A handful of good life,' says George Herbert, 'is worth a bushel of learning.' Not that learning is to be despised, but that it must be allied to goodness. Intellectual capacity is sometimes found associated with the meanest moral character with abject servility to those in high places, and arrogance to those of low estate. A man may be accomplished in art, literature, and science, and yet, in honesty, virtue, truthfulness, and the spirit of duty, be entitled to take rank after many a poor and illiterate peasant.

'You insist,' wrote Perthes to a friend, 'on respect for learned men. I say, Amen! But, at the same time, don't forget that largeness of mind, depth of thought, appreciation of the lofty, experience of the world, delicacy of manner, tact and energy in action, love of truth, honesty, and amiability— that all these may be wanting in a man who may yet be very learned.'

When someone, in Sir Walter Scott's hearing, made a remark as to the value of literary talents and accomplishments, as if they were above all things to be esteemed and honoured, he observed, 'God help us! what a poor world this would be if that were the true doctrine! I have read books enough, and observed and conversed with enough of eminent and splendidly-cultured minds, too, in my time; but I assure you, I have heard higher sentiments from the lips of poor uneducated men and women, when exerting the spirit of severe yet gentle heroism under difficulties and afflictions, or speaking their simple thoughts as to circumstances in the lot of friends and neighbours, than I ever yet met with out of the Bible. We shall never learn to feel and respect our real calling and destiny, unless we have taught ourselves to consider everything as moonshine, compared with the education of the heart.'

Still less has wealth any necessary connection with elevation of character. On the contrary, it is much more frequently the cause of its corruption and degradation. Wealth and corruption, luxury and vice, have very close affinities to each other. Wealth, in the hands of men of weak purpose, of deficient self-control, or of ill-regulated passions, is only a temptation and a snare—the source, it may be, of infinite mischief to themselves, and often to others.

On the contrary, a condition of comparative poverty is compatible with character in its highest form. A man may possess only his industry, his frugality, his integrity, and yet stand high in the rank of true manhood. The advice which Burns's father gave him was the best:

> *'He bade me act a manly part, though*
> *I had ne'er a farthing,*
> *For without an honest manly heart*
> *no man was worth regarding.'*

One of the purest and noblest characters the writer ever knew was a labouring man in a northern county, who brought up his family respectably on an income never amounting to more than ten shillings a week. Though possessed of only the rudiments of common education, obtained at an ordinary parish school, he was a man full of wisdom and thoughtfulness. His library consisted of the Bible, 'Flavel,' and 'Boston'—books which, excepting the first, probably few readers have ever heard of. This good man might have sat for the portrait of Wordsworth's well-known 'Wanderer.' When he had lived his modest life of work and worship, and finally went to his rest, he left behind him a reputation for practical wisdom, for genuine goodness, and for helpfulness in every good work, which greater and richer men might have envied.

Character is property. It is the noblest of possessions. It is an estate in the general goodwill and respect of men; and they who invest in it—though they may not become rich in this world's goods—will find their reward in esteem and reputation fairly and honourably won. And it is right that in life good qualities should tell—that industry, virtue, and goodness should rank the highest—and that the really best men should be foremost.

Talent is by no means rare in the world; nor is even genius. But can the talent be trusted?—can the genius? Not unless based on truthfulness—on veracity. It is this quality more than any other that commands the esteem and respect, and secures the confidence of others. Truthfulness is at the foundation of all personal excellence. It exhibits itself in conduct. It is rectitude—truth in action, and shines through every word and deed. It means reliableness, and convinces other men that it can be trusted. And a man is already of consequence in the world when it is known that he can be relied on—that when he says he knows a thing, he does know it—that when he says he will do a thing, he can do, and does it. Thus reliableness becomes a passport to the general esteem and confidence of mankind.

In the affairs of life or of business, it is not intellect that tells so much as character—not brains so much as heart—not genius so much as self-control, patience, and discipline, regulated by judgment. Hence there is no better provision for the uses of either private or public life, than a fair share of ordinary good sense guided by rectitude. Good sense, disciplined by experience and inspired by goodness, issues in practical wisdom. Indeed, goodness in a measure implies wisdom—the highest wisdom—the union of the worldly with the spiritual. 'The correspondences of wisdom and goodness,' says Sir Henry Taylor, 'are manifold; and that they will accompany each other is to be inferred, not only because men's wisdom makes them good, but because their goodness makes them wise.'

It is because of this controlling power of character in life that we often see men exercise an amount of influence apparently out of all proportion to their intellectual endowments. They appear to act by means of some latent power, some reserved force, which acts secretly, by mere presence. As Burke said of a powerful nobleman of the last century, 'his virtues were his means.' The secret is, that the aims of such men are felt to be pure and noble, and they act upon others with a constraining power.

Though the reputation of men of genuine character may be of slow growth, their true qualities cannot be wholly concealed. They may be misrepresented by some, and misunderstood by others; misfortune and adversity may, for a time, overtake them but, with patience and endurance, they will eventually inspire the respect and command the confidence which they really deserve.

Character is formed by a variety of minute circumstances, more or less under the regulation and control of the individual. Not a day passes without its discipline, whether for good or for evil. There is no act, however trivial, but has its train of consequences, as there is no hair so small but casts its shadow.

Character exhibits itself in conduct, guided and inspired by principle, integrity, and practical wisdom. In its highest form, it is the individual will acting energetically under the influence of religion, morality, and reason. It chooses its way considerately, and pursues it steadfastly; esteeming duty above reputation, and the approval of conscience more than the world's praise. While respecting the personality of others, it preserves its own individuality and independence; and has the courage to be morally honest, though it may be unpopular, trusting tranquilly to time and experience for recognition.

30

Swami Vivekananda

In the following passage, Swami Vivekananda, one of the greatest spiritual philosophers in the world, teaches us the crucial lesson of focussing on the means of work as much as the end. Highlighting the common human tendency to be drawn solely towards the ideal or goal, the text discusses the paradoxical nature of success, asserting that true happiness lies giving without expecting anything in return and cultivating 'superdivine' strength to navigate life's complexities.

~

WORK AND ITS SECRETS

One of the greatest lessons I have learnt in my life is to pay as much attention to the means of work as to its end. He was a great man from whom I learnt it, and his own life was a practical demonstration of this great principle. I have been always learning great lessons from that one principle, and it appears to me that all the secret of success is there; to pay as much attention to the means as to the end.

Our great defect in life is that we are so much drawn to the ideal, the goal is so much more enchanting, so much more alluring, so much bigger in our mental horizon, that we lose sight of the details altogether.

But whenever failure comes, if we analyse it critically, in ninety-nine per cent of cases we shall find that it was because we did not pay attention to the means. Proper attention to the finishing, strengthening, of the means is what we need. With the means all right, the end must come. We forget that it is the cause that produces the effect; the effect cannot come by itself;

and unless the causes are exact, proper, and powerful, the effect will not be produced. Once the ideal is chosen and the means determined, we may almost let go the ideal, because we are sure it will be there, when the means are perfected. When the cause is there, there is no more difficulty about the effect, the effect is bound to come. If we take care of the cause, the effect will take care of itself. The realization of the ideal is the effect. The means are the cause: attention to the means, therefore, is the great secret of life. We also read this in the Gita and learn that we have to work, constantly work with all our power; to put our whole mind in the work, whatever it be, that we are doing. At the same time, we must not be attached. That is to say, we must not be drawn away from the work by anything else; still, we must be able to quit the work whenever we like.

If we examine our own lives, we find that the greatest cause of sorrow is this: we take up something, and put our whole energy on it—perhaps it is a failure and yet we cannot give it up. We know that it is hurting us, that any further clinging to it is simply bringing misery on us; still, we cannot tear ourselves away from it. The bee came to sip the honey, but its feet stuck to the honey-pot and it could not get away. Again and again, we are finding ourselves in that state. That is the whole secret of existence. Why are we here? We came here to sip the honey, and we find our hands and feet sticking to it. We are caught, though we came to catch. We came to enjoy; we are being enjoyed. We came to rule; we are being ruled. We came to work; we are being worked. All the time, we find that. And this comes into every detail of our life. We are being worked upon by other minds, and we are always struggling to work on other minds. We want to enjoy the pleasures of life; and they eat into our vitals. We want to get everything from nature, but we find in the long run that nature takes everything from us—depletes us, and casts us aside.

Had it not been for this, life would have been all sunshine. Never mind! With all its failures and successes, with all its joys and sorrows, it can be one succession of sunshine, if only we are not caught.

That is the one cause of misery: we are attached, we are being caught. Therefore says the Gita: work constantly; work, but be not attached; be not caught. Reserve unto yourself the power of detaching yourself from everything, however beloved, however much the soul might yearn for it, however great the pangs of misery you feel if you were going to leave it; still, reserve the power of leaving it whenever you want. The weak have no place here, in this life or in any other life. Weakness leads to slavery. Weakness leads to all kinds of misery, physical and mental. Weakness is death. There are hundreds of thousands of microbes surrounding us, but they cannot harm us unless we become weak, until the body is ready and predisposed to receive them. There may be a million microbes of misery, floating about us. Never mind! They dare not approach us, they have no power to get a hold on us, until the mind is weakened. This is the great fact: strength is life, weakness is death. Strength is felicity, life eternal, immortal; weakness is constant strain and misery: weakness is death.

Attachment is the source of all our pleasures now. We are attached to our friends, to our relatives; we are attached to our intellectual and spiritual works; we are attached to external objects, so that we get pleasure from them. What, again, brings misery but this very attachment? We have to detach ourselves to earn joy. If only we had power to detach ourselves at will, there would not be any misery. That man alone will be able to get the best of nature, who, having the power of attaching himself to a thing with all his energy, has also the power to detach himself when he should do so. The difficulty is that there must be as much power of attachment as that of detachment. There are men who are never attracted by anything. They can never love, they are hard-hearted and apathetic; they escape most of the miseries of life. But the wall never feels misery, the wall never loves, is never hurt; but it is the wall, after all. Surely it is better to be attached and caught, than to be a wall. Therefore the man who never loves, who is hard and stony, escaping most of the miseries of life, escapes also its joys. We do not want that. That is weakness, that is death. That soul has not been awakened that never feels weakness, never feels misery. That is a callous state. We do not want that.

At the same time, we not only want this mighty power of love, this mighty power of attachment, the power of throwing our whole soul upon a single object, losing ourselves and letting ourselves be annihilated, as it were, for other souls—which is the power of the gods—but we want to be higher even than the gods. The perfect man can put his whole soul upon that one point of love, yet he is unattached. How comes this? There is another secret to learn.

The beggar is never happy. The beggar only gets a dole with pity and scorn behind it, at least with the thought behind that the beggar is a low object. He never really enjoys what he gets.

We are all beggars. Whatever we do, we want a return. We are all traders. We are traders in life, we are traders in virtue, we are traders in religion. And alas! we are also traders in love. If you come to trade, if it is a question of give-and-take, if it is a question of buy-and-sell, abide by the laws of buying and selling. There is a bad time and there is a good time; there is a rise and a fall in prices: always you expect the blow to come. It is like looking at the mirrors. Your face is reflected: you make a grimace—there is one in the mirror; if you laugh, the mirror laughs. This is buying and selling, giving and taking.

We get caught. How? Not by what we give, but by what we expect. We get misery in return for our love; not from the fact that we love, but from the fact that we want love in return. There is no misery where there is no want. Desire, want, is the father of all misery. Desires are bound by the laws of success and failure. Desires must bring misery.

The great secret of true success, of true happiness, then, is this: the man who asks for no return, the perfectly unselfish man, is the most successful. It seems to be a paradox. Do we not know that every man who is unselfish in life gets cheated, gets hurt? Apparently, yes. 'Christ was unselfish, and yet he was crucified.' True, but we know that his unselfishness is the reason, the cause of a great victory—the crowning of millions upon millions of lives with the blessings of true success.

Ask nothing; want nothing in return. Give what you have to give; it will come back to you—but do not think of that now, it will come back multiplied a thousandfold—but the attention must not be on that. Yet have the power to give: give, and there it ends. Learn that the whole of life is giving, that nature will force you to give. So, give willingly. Sooner or later you will have to give up. You come into life to accumulate. With clenched hands, you want to take. But nature puts a hand on your throat and makes your hands open. Whether you will it or not, you have to give. The moment you say, 'I will not', the blow comes; you are hurt. None is there but will be compelled, in the long run, to give up everything. And the more one struggles against this law, the more miserable one feels. It is because we dare not give, because we are not resigned enough to accede to this grand demand of nature, that we are miserable. The forest is gone, but we get heat in return. The sun is taking up water from the ocean, to return it in showers. You are a machine for taking and giving: you take, in order to give. Ask, therefore, nothing in return; but the more you give, the more will come to you. The quicker you can empty the air out of this room, the quicker it will be filled up by the external air; and if you close all the doors and every aperture, that which is within will remain, but that which is outside will never come in, and that which is within will stagnate, degenerate, and become poisoned. A river is continually emptying itself into the ocean and is continually filling up again. Bar not the exit into the ocean. The moment you do that, death seizes you.

Be, therefore, not a beggar; be unattached. This is the most terrible task of life! You do not calculate the dangers on the path. Even by intellectually recognising the difficulties, we really do not know them until we feel them. From a distance we may get a general view of a park: well, what of that? We feel and really know it when we are in it. Even if our every attempt is a failure, and we bleed and are torn asunder, yet, through all this, we have to preserve our heart—we must assert our Godhead in the midst of all these difficulties. Nature wants us to react, to return blow for blow, cheating for cheating, lie for lie, to hit back with all our might. Then it requires a superdivine power not to hit back, to keep control, to be unattached.

We are all the time, from our childhood, trying to lay the blame upon something outside ourselves. We are always standing up to set right other people, and not ourselves. If we are miserable, we say, 'Oh, the world is a devil's world.' We curse others and say, 'What infatuated fools!' But why should we be in such a world, if we really are so good? If this is a devil's world, we must be devils also; why else should we be here? 'Oh, the people of the world are so selfish!' True enough; but why should we be found in that company, if we be better? Just think of that.

Notes on Contributors

James Allen was born in 1864 to a working-class family in Leicester, England. Following the death of his father, he was forced to find work to support his family at the age of fifteen. Throughout the 1890s he worked as a secretary in a British manufacturing firm and later found a role in journalism. In 1898, he explored his interest in spirituality by writing for a magazine called the *Herald of the Golden Age*, and by 1902, he started his publication called *The Epoch*. *As a Man Thinketh*, published in 1903, is his third and most famous work. He continued writing until his death in 1912.

Arnold Bennett was a celebrated English novelist, playwright, and essayist, acclaimed for his diverse literary contributions that captured the essence of early twentieth-century society. His novels, including *The Old Wives' Tale*, *The Grand Babylon Hotel*, and the *Clayhanger* trilogy, showcased vivid realism and his acute observation of human nature, social dynamics, and the impact of modernity. As a chronicler of the times, he captured the transformations occurring in society during the transition from the Victorian era to the modern age. He died in 1931.

Olivia Ward Bush-Banks was an accomplished African American writer, journalist, and activist, who emerged as a notable figure during the early twentieth century. Bush-Banks displayed versatile talent, excelling as a playwright, novelist, and essayist. Her literary contributions addressed racial and gender issues, advocating for social change. Her notable works include *Dr. Pauline*, a novel exploring racism in the medical field, and *The Heir of Slaves*, a play shedding light on African–American experiences. A trailblazer for women of colour in literature, Bush-Banks left an indelible mark with her impactful writings and advocacy for social justice. She died in 1944.

Dale Carnegie was an American author and lecturer. He was born in poverty in Missouri in 1888. A skilful orator from a young age, Carnegie was active in his school debate team. He won several intercollegiate public speaking contests. He started his career as a salesman upon graduating from college in 1908. Following a brief stint as an actor in 1911, he taught his first public speaking course at the YMCA in New York. His courses soon became immensely popular and, by 1930, he began recruiting individuals to deliver courses in professional improvement throughout the country. He is considered a pioneer in self-improvement and his works including *How to Win Friends and Influence People* (1936) and *How to Stop Worrying and Start Living* (1948) are popular to this day. He died in 1955.

George Clason was an influential American writer and businessman, best known for his 1926 classic tract on financial growth and moneymaking, *The Richest Man in Babylon*. Born in Louisiana and a graduate of the University of Nebraska, Clason served in American army during the Spanish–American War and then went on to become a successful entrepreneur, founding the Clason Map Company and the Clason Publishing Company. His writings, blending wisdom with engaging storytelling, continue to inspire generations of readers who seek to cultivate fiscal responsibility. He died in 1957.

Emily Dickinson, an enigmatic American poet, born in Amherst, Massachusetts, remains a literary icon known for her unique voice and unconventional style. Despite a reclusive life, Dickinson's profound poems explored themes of nature, death, and the human soul. Her work, often characterized by unconventional punctuation and capitalization, challenged poetic norms. Although only a few of her nearly 1,800 poems were published during her lifetime, posthumously, she gained recognition as a major literary figure. Dickinson's introspective and emotionally charged verses continue to captivate. She died in 1886.

Kahlil Gibran is a Lebanese-American poet, philosopher, and visual artist, celebrated for his reflective writing that poetically captures complex emotions and explores poignant universal truths surrounding the human experience. His magnum opus, *The Prophet,* published in 1923, encapsulates his wisdom on life's fundamental aspects, such as love, pain, joy, and freedom. Gibran's words reflect a melange of his Eastern heritage and Western influences, creating a harmonious blend of mysticism and modernity that greatly appeal to those seeking solace and enlightenment. He died in 1931.

Henry Thomas Hamblin was a prominent British author and spiritual teacher known for his everlasting contributions to the New Thought Movement. His influential writings highlighted the power of positive thinking, self-discovery, and the alignment of one's thoughts with their desired reality. Hamblin's most renowned work, *The Power of Thought*, was published in 1921 and is today considered a cornerstone in the field of personal development and spiritual growth. Hamblin's teachings offered profound yet practical insights into harnessing the creative force of thoughts, continuing to inspire millions on their journeys of self-improvement and enlightenment. He died in 1958.

Napoleon Hill was an American motivational author. He was born in Virginia in 1883 and started writing at the age of thirteen. He is most famous for his work *Think and Grow Rich*, an all-time bestseller published in 1937. He established the Napoleon Hill Foundation, a non-profit institution that promotes his philosophy of personal achievement, leadership, and success. He died in 1970.

William George Jordan was a distinguished American essayist, editor, lecturer, and a notable figure in the development of self-improvement as a genre of literature. He was renowned for his insightful writings on personal growth, psychology, and leadership. He rose to prominence with books such as *The Majesty of Calmness* and *The Kingship of Self-control,* where he emphasized the significance of inner calm, self-discipline, and ethical living in a fast-paced world. He died in 1928.

Orison Swett Marden was a prominent American author and inspirational speaker whose writings have influenced countless people, from the common reader to presidents and business magnates. His teachings centre on personal development, the principles of success, and the power of a positive mindset. Marden's influential books, *Pushing to the Front* and *An Iron Will*, offered hands-on advice on achieving goals, overcoming obstacles through determination and self-discipline, and cultivating a strong character and unwavering optimism. It is believed that Marden's work laid the foundation for the self-help genre, inspiring generations to tap into their inner potential and lead fulfilling lives. He died in 1924.

Joseph Murphy was born in Ireland in 1898. He joined the Jesuits at an early age and began preparing to be initiated into the priesthood. However, he then decided to emigrate to America and became a pharmacist in New York City. He was interested in the study of different religions and travelled to India to learn about Asian religions. He later started his church in Los Angeles in the 1940s. He earned a PhD in psychology from the University of Southern California and wrote thirty books in the self-help genre. He died in 1981.

Earl Prevette, a highly successful salesman and author, hailed from North Carolina, where he earned his bachelor's degree from Wake Forest College in 1915 and graduated from Wake Forest Law School in 1919. Relocating to Philadelphia in 1920, he joined the Equitable Life Assurance Society and later worked with the Sun Life Assurance Co. of Canada from 1929 to 1952. He is best known for books on business and entrepreneurship like *How to Turn Your Ability into Cash*, *How to Sell by Telephone*, and *The Power of Creative Selling*.

Arthur Schopenhauer was a German philosopher best known for his 1818 publication, *The World as Will and Representation*. Schopenhauer's philosophy often spoke of transcending individual desires to escape the cycles of suffering through contemplation, aesthetics, and asceticism. Schopenhauer's ideas significantly influenced later philosophers, particularly Friedrich Nietzsche and Jean-Paul Sartre. His unique perspective on the human condition continues to stimulate debates about the nature of existence and the potential for attaining a form of liberation from the relentless cycle of desire. He died in 1860.

Samuel Smiles was a Scottish author, government reformer, and physician, best remembered for his pioneering work in the self-help genre. Born in Haddington, Scotland, Smiles gained prominence in 1859 with the publication of his influential book, *Self-help*, advocating personal responsibility, perseverance, and thrift as keys to success. His writings aimed to inspire individuals to overcome adversity and improve their lives through hard work and self-discipline. Smiles's impact extended beyond literature, as he contributed to social reform efforts and held various public positions. He died in 1904.

Lucian B. Watkins was born in 1879 in Chesterfield, Virginia. He attended local public schools and later studied at Virginia Normal and Industrial Institute in Petersburg. A schoolteacher turned poet, he published *Voices of Solitude* in 1903 and *The Old Log Cabin* in 1910. He gained prominence for his poem *The Star of Ethiopia* (1918), dedicated to W. E. B. Du Bois. Serving in World War I, Watkins wrote about his experiences, capturing the irony of facing danger in both the American South and foreign war zones. Anthologized posthumously, Watkins may have been the first enlisted African–American soldier to publish a book of poetry. He died in 1921.

Swami Vivekananda was a nineteenth-century philosopher, nationalist, and monk credited with introducing Vedanta philosophy, modern Hindu thought, and yoga to the Western world in the Parliament of World's Religions in Chicago in 1893. Born as Narendranath Datta in an influential Bengali family in Calcutta, Swami Vivekananda found himself drawn to spirituality and religion from an early age. In November 1881, he met Sri Ramakrishna—a turning point in his life—who would show him the path to realize God through renunciation, prayer, and selfless service of one's fellow men. In his teacher's final days, Swami Vivekananda received ochre robes and was asked to lead the monastic brotherhood known as the Ramakrishna Math. On 4 July 1902, he died while meditating in the monastery at Belur Math.